Fell's Guide to

Hand Puppets:

How To Make and Use Them

Fell's Guide to

Hand Puppets:

How To Make and Use Them

by

Dorothy Richter

A World of Books That Fill a Need

Frederick Fell, Inc.   *New York*

PN 1972
. R5
1970
Cop. 1

Copyright © 1970 by Dorothy Richter

For information address:
Frederick Fell, Inc.
386 Park Avenue South
New York, N.Y. 10016

Library of Congress Catalog Card No. 78-91101

Published simultaneously in Canada by
George J. McLeod, Limited, Toronto 2B, Ontario

Manufactured in the United States of America

Standard Book Number 8119-0185-8

To Betty, for not letting me go off on tangents, and Jule, for relieving me of KP while I wrote this book.

Acknowledgment

I wish to express my appreciation to the people who made this book possible: my daughter, Juliann, for illustrating the book; my good friend Marianne, for typing it; the expert help of the public library staff; and the many friends whose encouragement meant so much.

Contents

Introduction

In this hurry-up workaday world in which we live, there are all too few chances to be creative. When we do find time, there are those who will say, "What can I do without art training?"

You can make puppets; they are within the capabilities of most of us.

The truth of this statement was demonstrated by a friend, who, with no previous art experience, made delightful puppets by following the instructions in this book. The puppets were sent to a young nephew who lives abroad. When he and his parents came to visit recently, seven-year-old Steve's first question was, "Can we make Charlie Brown and Snooky puppets, Aunt Betty?"

They did.

You may have a very different reason for making puppets; they have so many uses.

Teaching classes in school, Sunday school, or summer camp may be your reason. If you are a member of a church group, school PTA, or woman's club and need to raise money, a puppet play is a solution. If your aim is to give pleasure to patients in hospitals, children in day-care centers, library groups, or to the elderly, retarded, or handicapped, there is no better way than with puppets.

If you are not part of a group but are groping for a means of giving pleasure to shut-ins and others, you can give an effective performance with a walking stage and a puppet on either hand. How easily one could relieve the monotony of hospital patients or put on a performance that the Golden Age Club would long remember.

The production of a puppet play is especially suited to group activity because it offers a wide choice of assignments. No one need be left out. In addition to sculptors and painters, there is work for a seamstress and for those interested in writing, directing, and promoting. Husbands can be drawn into the activity as carpenters, electricians, and stagehands. In this do-it-yourself age, you may find a husband with a home workshop who will construct the puppet stage. He may even make such welcome additions as a wind machine and puppet furniture.

When the puppets and stage are completed and the play rehearsed, the show is ready to go anywhere at any time. The difficulties of putting on a play with many human actors are practically eliminated with some puppets. They never get sick, never have temper tantrums; their costumes are inexpensive to make and are easy to transport. The same puppets can be used for adult performances as are used to entertain children by adapting the script to the audience.

A puppet theater in the home draws the family together, from the smallest child to the oldest adult, in a single purpose. I recently visited a home in which the children were working on the production of a puppet play as a summer activity. Their interest had been triggered by a professional puppet show on the school lyceum program. However, children need very little encouragement where puppets are concerned. They are naturally fascinated by a fantasy world in which animals talk, people fly, and creatures never before seen do impossible things.

These children chose to produce Bil Baird's *Magic Onion*. In no time the whole family was involved. The puppets were finished and so was a simple stage made of a large piece of corrugated cardboard donated by a furniture store. The cardboard had been bent into a three-part screen with a stage opening cut in the front. They painted it green. A sprinkling of psychedelic flower decals brightened the front.

The day I visited they were discussing the performance which was to be given in the backyard, weather permitting, or in the garage in event of rain. The question being debated was whether to charge admission. I don't know the outcome of the argument, but I knew that they would be occupied with puppets for some time to come and I hoped they would be able to carry their interest over to school in the fall.

I remember the wonderful rapport in my sixth-, seventh-, and eighth-grade classes in puppetry during the past year; the contributions of cloth, fur, buttons, bits of lace, beads and felt that made possible the fanciful costumes; the very fine modeling on the head of a devil made by a boy who ordinarily did nothing for which he could be praised; the sixth-grade boy who invented a contraption which opened and closed the mouth of his sea serpent puppet. There was Beth whose beguiling gray mouse with broomstraw whiskers and pink felt ears was her dearest possession. She took it home with her every night for safekeeping.

All of the time that they were making puppet heads and clothes, writing plays, rehearsing, and painting backdrops, they were training their eyes, voices, hands, and minds. They were being creative in every sense of the word, which was a great satisfaction to me because mass education tends to develop conformity. There was no conformity here. They were extraordinarily ingenious with the materials at hand; their ideas were fresh and sincere, and the puppet performances were delightfully naive.

Puppet plays are an excellent way of linking different school subjects. For example, in order to put on a play with a historical background, research must be done—geography, language, customs, and dress. It is possible to revive a lagging interest in a subject with the use of puppets. Dramatization makes the subject more inviting.

Puppets are also a means of teaching good standards of social behavior without being preachy. Children are much more impressed by a good visual lesson than by any amount of reading. When Peter Puppet advises the regular use of a toothbrush or warns against crossing the street without looking, the advice is more apt to be heeded.

Puppets are most useful in "bringing out" the shy

child. I recall little Tim in second grade who spoke haltingly with eyes downcast and then only rarely. He became quite eloquent under cover of the puppet stage as the father of Hansel and Gretel. Drunk with the power of his new-found verbosity but running out of rehearsed script, he declaimed on the weather, his wife's poor housekeeping, and the behavior of his children. Only when he had completely run out of subject matter did he relinquish the spotlight.

Puppets are most useful in therapy and rehabilitation work with adults and children. Wheelchair patients can have a simple theater attached to the chair or a simple stage can be rigged upon a bed. An appreciative audience is a very good morale-builder and a means of taking the mind off one's self by giving pleasure to others. It is a two-way thing. Children in the audience are often drawn into the play to the extent of talking back to the puppets.

Patients with physical disabilities such as arthritis or an injured hand that needs exercise will enjoy operating a hand puppet.

Since puppetry is a group activity and needs an audience, it can help the psychoneurotic to draw out of his shell. Scripts dealing with situations and problems with which they can identify teach them that others have problems too, and the problems are not insurmountable. When using puppets as psychotherapy, it is best to work with a trained therapist since harm as well as good could result.

An awakening is taking place to the potentialities of puppets as a means of enriching the school curriculum.

Puppets are being taken seriously. Their use is being explored in many areas. At least one educator is offering a set of puppets along with basic reading programs. Speech therapists are using puppets in their field, and puppet films are used to teach such subjects as mathematics and foreign languages. Puppetry has been used for a long time in Mexico as an educational tool. It is being used to improve literacy and public health and to acquaint the people with their historical background.

India also is aware of the educational value of puppets. When Bil Baird, one of the leading puppeteers in this country, was traveling in India with his puppet company, he worked with people from all over India to prepare plays on such subjects as smallpox inoculation versus the witch doctor, family planning, and child marriage. Flying squads of puppets go into villages to help with problems. The puppets are being produced in a number of places in India.

Puppets are also being used in education in Argentina, Uruguay, and Chile. Even the governments of Communist countries are aware of not only the educational value of puppets but of their attitude-forming power. Since the theater is a part of the educational system, the government has a certain amount of control over subject matter; hence, emphasis is on attitude-building.

Puppets once considered only for their entertainment value have proved their worth in other fields as well. In other words, puppets are here to stay.

Fell's Guide to

Hand Puppets:

How To Make and Use Them

Chapter 1.

A Brief History
of Puppets

Puppets have been around a long time, probably as long as man. To find their beginning, we would have to go beyond recorded history.

Puppets have been found in Egyptian tombs that were more than three thousand years old. From ancient Greece and later from Rome, small jointed figures used in religious rituals have survived. There are references to figures worked by strings in writings of such classical scholars as Aristotle, Horace, and Plato.

Puppets also existed in the early history of India, China, Japan, Java, and Burma, and they are still a popular form of entertainment in these countries. There is a curious relationship between the shadow puppet and the human actor in Java. Facial expressions, head-dresses, costumes, and even the side-to-side movement of the human dancer are imitations of puppets.

As a form of entertainment puppets are at least as old as the theater itself. Puppet shows were known in ancient Greece in the fifth century B.C.

Since medieval times puppets have been used in western Europe as a means of entertainment. Strolling players performed on the streets, at fairs, in inns and in the marketplace. Eventually permanent theaters were established for the common people as well as for royalty, who had their own private theaters.

At first, plays were restricted to religious subjects. Later, tales of chivalry and satirical plays were performed. In the eighteenth century, comedy was introduced and the comic figure evolved. He was a clown type, a country bumpkin with a hooked nose who was in turn merry, boastful, cowardly, and quick-tempered. He appeared first in Italy, where he was known as Pulcinella; in Russia, as Petruchka; in Germany, as Kasperl; and in England, as Punch.

Many famous people were in some way connected with puppets. Haydn composed operas for marionettes; George Bernard Shaw wrote plays for them; George Sand and her son Maurice founded the Théatre des Amis in her home, where they produced witty and satirical hand-puppet plays for friends. At one time their puppets numbered eight hundred.

Puppetry had an early beginning in America. Before the white man came, the Indians of New Mexico and the northwest coast used puppets of a sort which they manipulated by hidden strings to awe their tribesmen during religious ceremonies. These secret rites are still practiced today.

Cortez brought the first known European puppeteer with him during his conquest of Mexico in the sixteenth century.

Later in colonial America, an occasional puppet play was performed by English, French, or Spanish puppeteers. There are records of puppet shows being performed in New York in 1738 and in Philadelphia in 1742.

But puppet performances were rare until the nineteenth century when immigrants began arriving from Europe. They brought their puppet heritages with them. Puppet plays were generally given for audiences from the same national origins as the puppeteers. The second-generation English, French, Germans, and Italians had no interest in puppets, and the art dwindled. By 1900, puppet shows had all but disappeared.

A revival of interest took place around 1915 when a new kind of puppet play was created by artists and people of culture. These plays were given for their friends. Some were so popular that they became professional.

Among those that pioneered in the revival of puppetry were Tony Sarg, Ellen Van Vockenburg, and Remo Bufano.

The interest in puppets grew and broadened. In 1937, the Puppeteers of America was founded. Except for a lapse during World War II, the organization of amateurs, professionals, and educators have met to further the growth of interest in the puppet theater. Today there are puppet companies, large and small, traveling and in permanent theaters all over the country. One permanent theater has a staff of 220 persons to manage the puppet population of over a thousand. Some companies make motion pictures; others perform in night-clubs, theaters, and on television. Some specialize in commercial advertising.

Television brought puppets to millions of viewers. There was Edgar Bergen and his rollicking Charlie Mc-Carthy; followed by Burr Tillstroms' Kuklapolitans; Topo Gigio, the Italian mouse; and Shari Lewis and her puppets. Jim Hensen regularly presents his troupe of strange characters, The Moppets. The big variety shows on TV employ a number of puppet acts and plays each year. One of the best plays to appear was Bil Baird's *Peter and The Wolf*.

The industrial uses of puppets have also grown steadily. At the Chicago Century of Progress in 1934, marionettes told the story of refrigeration from prehistoric days to the modern refrigerator. Remo Bufano's marionettes enacted the story of the pharmacy at the New York World's Fair in 1940. And in 1964 and 1965, at the New York World's Fair, the Chrysler Corporation put on continuous shows for twelve hours a day—eighty-eight shows.

The puppet is an ideal advertising method whether used on TV or in store window displays. Puppets are used to sell underwear, soap, soup, and bathing suits.

Chapter 2.

The Puppet Head

The head is the most important as well as time-consuming part of the hand puppet. Though there are several ways of making puppet heads, the direct-modeling method has the advantage of being quick, simple, and most satisfying to the amateur puppetmaker.

The procedure is simple. The modeling media is molded into an egg shape around a cardboard tube that forms the neck. Features are modeled with fingers and simple makeshift tools such as an orangewood stick, toothpick, spoon handle or nail file. Then the head is dried, sanded, and painted.

The first step is the preparation of the sawdust and wallpaper-paste mixture. Fine sawdust produces better results than coarse. Sift the sawdust through a flour sifter for small amounts; for larger quantities, make a simple sifter by nailing together a wooden frame over which a fine screen is tacked.

Mix 4 cups of sifted sawdust with 1½ cups of dry wallpaper paste. Add enough water to make a pliable mixture that will hold its shape. This amount will make four to six heads depending on their size. It will keep for some time because wallpaper paste contains a preservative.

Now you are ready to make the head of a hand puppet. As the name implies, it is operated on the hand. It consists of a head and loose garment. Hand puppets usually have no legs; if they do, the legs dangle.

The index finger fits into the neck and hollow head. Thumb and forefinger fit into the sleeves; the garment conceals the hand (Fig. 1). In order to operate a hand puppet, the head must be hollow and lightweight. This

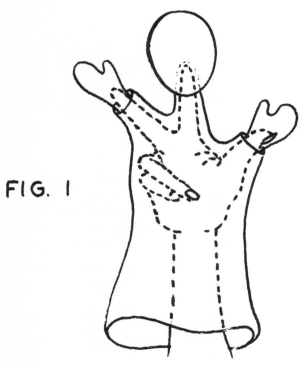

FIG. 1

is accomplished by rolling a piece of 4 inch by 6 inch
lightweight cardboard loosely around the index finger
and taping it in several places. A toilet paper tube slit
lengthwise, rolled to size, and secured with tape, saves
time. The tube will be too long but do not cut it off
now. It serves as a handle while modeling.

Take a lump of sawdust mixture about the size of a
baseball. Press it firmly into an egg shape. Force the
cardboard tube into the mixture slightly in back of the
pointed end and about halfway into the head (Fig. 2).
Withdraw the tube, shake out particles of the mixture,
and reinsert into the head. Pat a ¼-inch wall about 1
inch long on the tube, joining the head to form a neck.

If the mixture cracks, add water sparingly by damp-
ening the hands and rubbing the surface. Clip a clothespin on the mouth of a bottle filled with sand. Slip the
cardboard tube over the clothespin while modeling and

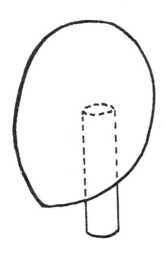

FIG. 2

drying the head. The mixture flattens when the head is allowed to lie in a prone position.

You are ready to create a puppet personality. You may wish to change the shape of the head by squeezing in here and building out there. The head can be an exaggerated pear shape, round, heart-shaped, or long and thin. A low receding forehead suggests a low mentality; a high forehead a brainy character (Fig. 3).

The head of a child can be done with very little modeling—just the hint of a nose and more space given to the upper part of the head than would normally be allowed for an adult (Fig. 4).

Keep in mind while you work that an effective puppet has "carrying power," which means that small details are omitted. The modeling is bold, and the features are simplified and exaggerated.

But you must know where and how the features are located before taking liberties with them.

To locate the features make a light vertical line with an orangewood stick down the middle of the face from top to bottom. Draw a horizontal line midway from the top of the head to the chin for placement of eyes. Halfway between the eye line and the bottom of the chin, make a mark for the tip of the nose. Divide the remaining space into three equal parts. The mouth fits into the middle space. The top of the ears are in line with the eyebrows; the tip of the ears are in line with the tip of the nose (Fig. 5).

After modeling a head or two, this marking will be unnecessary. The tendency is to place the eyes too high and the mouth too low.

FIG. 3

If hair is to be painted on later, provide for it now by adding extra modeling material in the style of your choice.

The head is ready for features. Begin by making eye sockets. With your thumb or a spoon handle placed on the eye-level line make slight indentations on either side of the vertical line; the upper ridge helps to place the eyebrows.

For a nose, pinch a bit of modeling material into a wedge shape. Moisten the spot where it is to be applied and press firmly in place. Roll two small marbles of the mixture and press on either side of the nose for nostrils. When working with small bits of mixture, moistening the fingers prevents stickiness.

To make the eyes and mouth, pat out three almond-shaped pieces ¼-inch thick and ¾-inch long. Apply to the

FIG. 4

moistened eye sockets and mouth area. The eyes should be the width of an eye apart (Fig. 6).

There is less danger of breaking off the ears if they are applied after the modeling is finished.

When you have become familiar with the placing of features, you may not find it necessary to cut out and apply eyes, nose and mouth. Instead you will pinch out here and push in there for the desired effect. If you

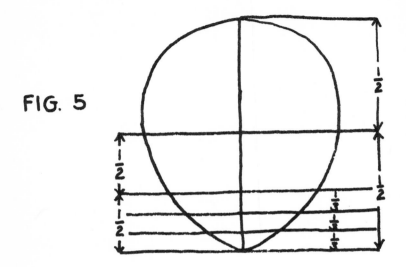

FIG. 5

have confidence in your own ability, you may prefer to begin modeling by the latter method.

Now you can explore ways of giving more character to your puppet head. The only limitation will be your imagination. Is this little actor to be sad, happy, ugly, beautiful, thin, or fat? Should the nose be large or small, hooked, upturned, or bulbous? Are the eyes to be large or small, close together or far apart? Will the mouth be open or closed, upturned or drooping? How about the ears? Are they to be large or small, close to the head, sticking out? Experiment. "Up" lines make for a happy expression; "down" lines produce a sad character (Fig. 7).

Perhaps you do not wish to make a realistic or semi-realistic puppet. You need a grotesque puppet—a moon

Chapter 3.

Animal Puppet Heads

All kinds of animals can be made as hand puppets. The most effective ones emphasize the essential characteristics, making them animal caricatures.

A wolf should have a lean and hungry look with the length of snout and teeth exaggerated. A fawn should

FIG. 8

express gentleness and have large appealing eyes. A puppet cannot exhibit more than one characteristic, which should be immediately apparent (Fig. 8).

The first thing to determine when creating an animal puppet is whether it will walk erect or on four feet. The head on an upright animal is positioned on the cardboard tube the same as for a person (Fig. 9). If it appears to walk in a horizontal position, the head comes out of the end of the tube as illustrated in Figure 10.

FIG. 9

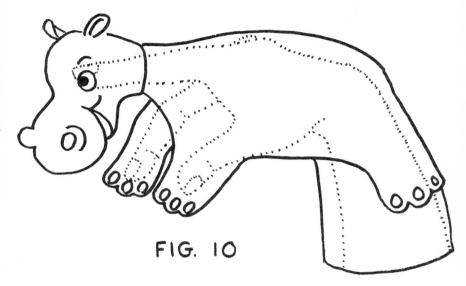

FIG. 10

Animal puppets are of two varieties: those with short snouts and bills that can be modeled in the same manner as people puppets, and those with long snouts or bills. The latter need props to extend the front of the face.

Excellent extenders for horses, bears, foxes, and fowl, such as the duck, are the dividers from egg cartons (Fig. 11).

Cut a dome-shaped divider from a carton. Press it into the wet sawdust mixture that has been balled around a cardboard tube. Build a thin wall of the mixture over the prop, re-shaping to suit the particular need (Fig. 12).

To make an open bill or snout, cut the prop down the

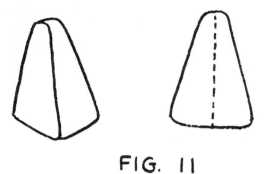

FIG. 11

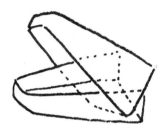

middle lengthwise. Press the halves into the face at the angle necessary for a wide open or slightly open mouth (Fig. 13).

Coat the inside of an animal's mouth with sawdust mixture and while wet, press in teeth made of cardboard, styrofoam, toothpicks, cork, or bits of a plastic bottle. Add the tongue at this time. Felt works well.

An elephant head, because of the trunk, requires a different kind of prop. Twist several long pipe cleaners together around a cardboard tube. Be sure they are

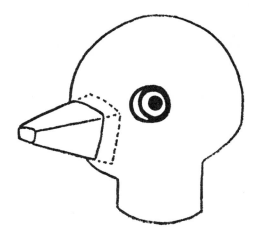

FIG. 12

FIG. 13

tight and will not slip. Bend the prop into the position
the trunk will take (Fig. 14). Apply sawdust mixture to
the head area and cover the trunk, squeezing firmly onto
the pipe cleaners.

Small ears can be made of the sawdust mixture when
the head is being modeled. For the larger ears of ele-
phants, donkeys, and rabbits, use felt. Slits or holes
should be made in the wet mixture for ears that will be

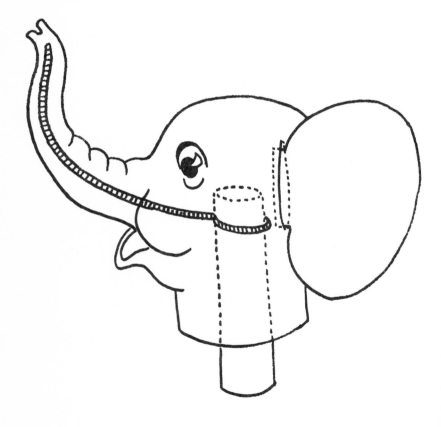

FIG. 14

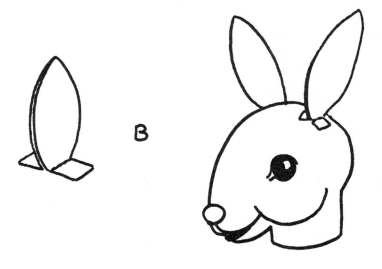

B

FIG. 15

A

glued in after the head has been painted (Fig. 15-A).

There is another method of applying ears which does not require puncturing the head. Cut four ear shapes of felt, making them ¼-inch longer than needed; glue two together up to the ¼-inch mark. When dry, apply glue to the flange, bend at right angles to the ear and press into position on the head (Fig. 15-B).

Ears can also be made of six layers of newspaper put together with wallpaper paste. Cut and shape ears while paper is wet.

Eyes can also be modeled of the sawdust mixture or they can be imbedded beads, buttons, marbles, or glass reflectors. Wiggle-eyes in several sizes are available in craft shops.

Eyes may hold if pressed into the wet sawdust head and allowed to dry, but it is safer to make the indentations and then remove them. After the head has been painted, glue the eyes into the sockets with epoxy or another strong adhesive.

If marbles are used, embed them half of their diameter deep. Eyelids can be modeled over the marble. Eyelashes of heavy thread or yarn dipped in glue and shaped before drying may be pushed into the wet eyelid with tweezers.

String, rope, yarn, felt pipe cleaners, and fringe are suitable tail or mane materials. Rope that is frayed at one end is especially good for a cow or lion tail.

A play may call for a puppet that can open and close its mouth, as in the play "Fisherman's Luck," pp. 159. The easiest puppet of this type to make is a sock puppet. Make it as follows:

Turn a man's sock inside out. Flatten the foot, heel down, on a table. Slit the toe from side to side (Fig. 16-A). The deeper the slit, the bigger the mouth. Fold the top half of the mouth back. Slip a folded piece of paper under the sock with the fold of the paper in line with the folded edge of the mouth (16-B). Trace around the lower half of the mouth. Remove the paper and cut out the mouth pattern. Trace the pattern on a piece of red, pink, or orange felt. Line up the felt mouth on the sock mouth, pin in place and sew around the oval mouth (16-C). Machine stitching will hold better than hand sewing on a loosely knit stretchy sock. As an added precaution, overcast the edge. Turn the sock right side out.

Using the mouth pattern, cut a piece of stiff cardboard. Trim off a ¼-inch margin all around. Fold across the middle (16-D). Slip the cardboard inside of the sock down into the mouth; the upper part of the cardboard is for the upper jaw, the lower half for the lower jaw. For hand position see Figure 33.

A sock puppet is versatile. The size, shape, and position of the ears, size of mouth, and shape of nose make possible a variety of animals. It might be a horse, dog, fish, crocodile, or dragon with the addition of a mane, tail, feathers, or teeth.

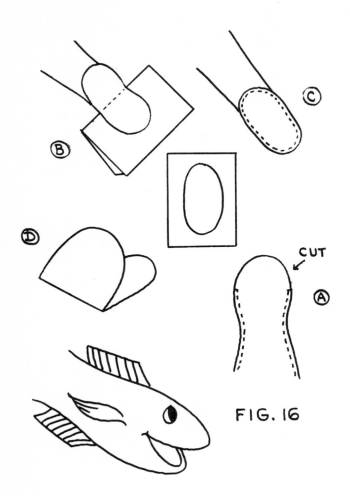

CUT

Ⓒ

Ⓑ

Ⓓ

Ⓐ

FIG. 16

Chapter 4.

Painting the Head

Heads can be painted with oil, acrylic, or tempera paints.

Oil paint gives a durable finish but takes longer than the others to dry. The shine can be cut down by adding a little French chalk to the paint or by spraying the finished head with a commercial matte medium.

Acrylic paint is a plastic waterproof paint. It can be thinned with water or a matte medium to control the degree of gloss.

Tempera is recommended for the beginner. It is a fast-drying, opaque, water-based paint. It is available in large or small jars or tubes and in powdered form. Jars or tubes are recommended.

Buy a large jar of white; it is the basis for skin color. You will need small jars of red, yellow, orange, brown, and blue.

For a basic flesh color, take a rounded teaspoon of white, which is enough for one head. Add a bit of red and orange, and mix well. Then add a touch of brown to tone down the color. Experiment with the amounts of color. There is no one skin color that is right for every type. Youthful characters need fresh bright colors; for older characters, gray the color slightly by adding a touch of blue.

Freckles on children's faces are painted with skin color to which brown has been added. Make them large enough to be seen from a distance and add them sparingly over the nose and upper cheeks. The same slightly darkened skin color can also be used to paint the inner ear and nostrils.

Vary the color of different races by adding yellow to the basic skin color for orientals, brown or black for the Negro, and red for the Indian.

The consistency of the paint is important. It must not be too thick. Add water gradually until it can be easily spread yet covers well. A thick coat is not necessary and tends to develop a network of fine cracks when dry. If this happens, dip a small piece of cloth in water and rub well, wiping off the excess paint. Paint will also crack if it is applied to a head that is not completely dry.

Apply the flesh color to the head and neck except for the hair area and eyes.

Blend pink or red on the cheeks while the paint is still wet. Wrinkles and lines of a deeper skin color should be painted on with bold strokes.

For visibility, the coloring must be more vivid than is natural. Color tends to wash out under bright lights.

When the flesh color is dry, paint in the features starting with the eyes. Rest your hand against the table edge for support when doing the precise painting of features. Paint the iris first, the pupil next, and then the white of the eye. The eye lines are last; the upper line should be heavier than the lower line. An upper lid of green, blue or lavender is a pleasing touch to the heads of some puppets. For the best effect, study the head under strong artificial light.

When the eye paint is dry, paint in a white highlight, to add a professional touch. This is a small white dot or triangle on the edge of the pupil either on the top or at the side (Fig. 17).

If eyebrows are to be painted instead of being made of fur, yarn, or other material, make them expressive. They can heighten the look of happiness, sorrow, surprise, or anger by their position—dipped down, straight, or highly arched. They can be thin and graceful or shaggy and beetling.

Paint the lips last to avoid smearing. For a realistic look, blend red with brown for the upper lip, which

FIG. 17

should be darker. The lower lip can be pure red or red with a touch of white. Paint the lips of children a shade lighter than those of older people.

If your first attempt at painting features is not satisfactory, wipe the paint off with a damp cloth and start again.

A grotesque head will dictate its own particular color needs. Its skin color may be white, green, blue, or any color you choose to paint it.

Painting the animal head differs very little from painting the human head. Cartoon characters on TV will give you many ideas for simplification of the features.

A head painted with tempera should be waterproofed and protected from chipping. This can be done by spraying with several coats of commercial lacquer, plastic from a pressurized can, or hair lacquer. You can make fixative by mixing one part of white shellac with two parts of denatured alcohol. Apply with an atomizer or insect spray gun.

Chapter 5.

Hair, Brows, Mustaches, and Beards

Hair, brows, mustache, and beard can be painted on the head, but they are generally more effective when made of yarn, hemp, chenille, thread, fur, rope, pipe cleaners, embroidery floss, sponge rubber, copper pot-cleaners—whatever best suits the character.

Hair can be glued directly to the head, sewed to fabric and then applied to the head, or sewed to a hat brim.

When applied directly to the head, glue rows of yarn, or other material, around the head starting at the base of the neck and working up to the top of the head. Make the first row longer than needed so that you can style the hair later. Each succeeding row should reach the bottom row.

Using this method, practically any type of hair arrangement can be created. This is especially suited to women's hair styles. For a bouffant effect, bring the two front rows on the forehead backward over loosely wadded hair material. This creates a high teased appearance

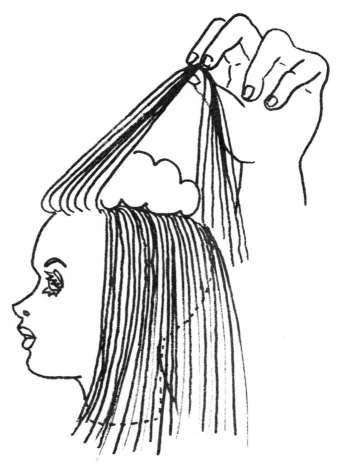

FIG. 17 - A

(Fig. 17-A). Bangs, buns, or braids are additional possibilities.

When hair is sewn to cloth before glueing to the head, the cloth is cut in a circle large enough to cover the hair area. Three slits are made in from the edge toward the center. Edges of the slits are overlapped as much as necessary to form a cap that fits the head. A sock heel can also be used. You will need to cut slots out of other side of the sock or cloth cap to accommodate the ears. With a darning needle threaded with a long strand of hair material, take a small stitch at the edge of the cap. Pull the hair through to the desired length and cut off a double strand. Repeat the small stitches until the entire cap is covered with a dense growth of "hair" (Fig. 18).

Another method uses a strip of cloth or felt ½-inch

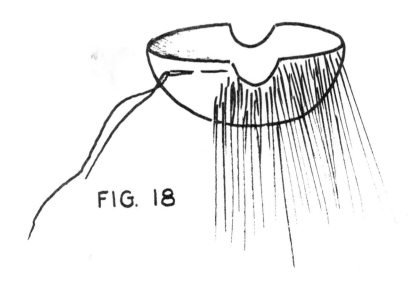

FIG. 18

wide and long enough to reach from the center of the hairline on the forehead to the nape of the neck. Cut the strands of "hair" the desired length and lay them across the strip on their halfway mark as close together as possible. Sew by hand or machine down the middle of the strip (Fig. 19). With this method it is best to glue bits of the hair material directly to the sides and back of the head before glueing the strip down the middle of the head.

A comic hairpiece can be made by wrapping yarn around the thumb and index finger. Tie the yarn in the middle, slip from the fingers, and cut both ends. Glue to the top of the head (Fig. 20).

Hair attached to the hat brim is useful if the puppet is to double as two characters. Sew the "hair" to a narrow band of cloth that fits around the inside of the hat

FIG. 19

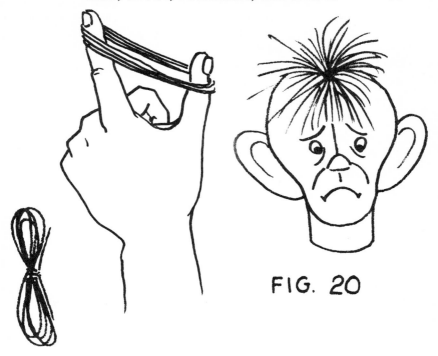

FIG. 20

brim. The "hair" can be cut in bangs, pulled back on either side from a center part or cut man-style (Fig. 21).

Fur is a versatile material as useful for the hair of people as it is for animals. A bag of scrap pieces of lamb's wool, dyed bright colors, is available through a craft catalogue listed in the section on Sources for Supplies.

Fur should be cut with a single-edge razor on the skin side. It is easier to glue small patches of fur to the head than to glue on larger pieces. Very narrow strips can be cut to serve as eyelashes, eyebrows, sideburns, beards, and mustaches.

Frayed rope or binder twine can be used as witches' hair. Black dyed Turkish toweling or bits of sponge rubber glued to the head and painted black serve as Negro hair. Copper pot cleaners make effective hair on a stylized angel.

A word about hair color: Under stage lights, bright shades of yellow, pink, or orange suggest blond hair. Shades of red, red-orange, or rust suggest red hair. The darker shades of purple, dark blue or green give the effect of black hair.

FIG. 21

Chapter 6.

The Costume

The costume is an important part of the over-all look of the puppet. It helps to give character to your creation, and it assists in distinguishing one puppet from another.

An important consideration when selecting fabric is that it must stand out against the background. Many a lovely costume has melted into the scenery.

If the puppet is to have much use, consider the durability of the fabric. A heavy material may wear better and help to disguise the fact that the puppeteer's hand is the puppet's body. Felt, corduroy, wool, gabardine, duck, twill, and cotton velvet are suitable materials. If the lighter-weight materials such as gingham are used, padding the shoulders and front with plastic foam helps to give the illusion of a body. In no case should the costume be so stiff that it impedes movement.

Texture is also important. Rough, smooth, dull, and shiny surfaces give variety, as do pattern and color. Small patterns are in keeping with the size of the puppet but not all carry well. There are way-out characters that need bold patterns and loud colors to emphasize their difference. But it would be a mistake to dress all the puppets in a play in bold patterns and bright colors of equal strength. They would lose their impact.

If the right pattern and color cannot be found, paint your own material. Block print, stencil, crayon, spatter, or silk-screen a design. There are many books with simple instructions for textile printing. Printing your own design is especially useful when dressing animal puppets. Scales, stripes, spots, or feather effects are possibilities.

Before you can cut a pattern for the costume, you must decide how you will manipulate your puppet. It will affect the pattern.

There are five or more possible hand positions. The accompanying illustrations explain the two most commonly used. The one shown in Figure 22-A is probably the most used and is especially good for picking up objects. The neck is mobile but when it is turned, the whole body turns. In Figure 22-B, the head turns freely without the body moving by moving the fingers inside of the neck.

The following costume is planned for a puppet operated by the finger positions shown in Figure 22-A.

Place your hand on a piece of paper and draw around the thumb and first two fingers with a generous margin (Fig. 23). Remove your hand and extend the lines to make a skirt, which should be no longer than your forearm. An exception would be diaphanous clothing that would need extra length in order to float and swirl.

Allow an extra ¼ inch around the drawing for seams and 1½ inches for a hem. Cut out the pattern and pin

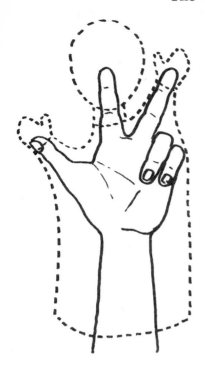

FIG. 22-A

it onto a double thickness of cloth with the right sides turned in. Cut out and sew as indicated on the dotted lines. Sew the hem, then turn the costume inside out. This is a removable costume.

Another version of the removable costume is made by cutting the neck straight, instead of tapered, and a little longer than for the previous costume. It must be

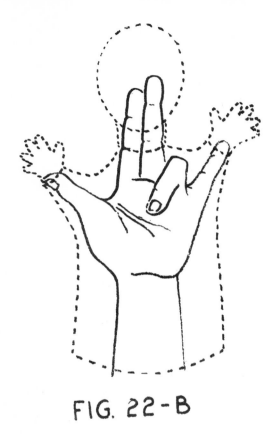

FIG. 22-B

slightly longer than the puppet neck after it is sewed. The top of the neck is left open (Fig. 24).

To join the costume and head, place a strong rubber band high on the puppet's neck. Work the rubber band down onto the cloth which is then turned down over the rubber band to make a turtleneck.

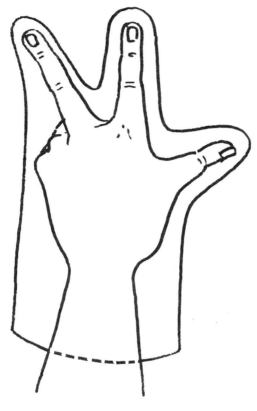

FIG. 23

If the costume is to be permanently attached to the head, cut the same as the one illustrated in Figure 24, except shorten the neck a bit. The neck must fit snugly in order to glue it onto the puppet neck.

The basic costume can be made more attractive by the addition of collars, cuffs, belts, buttons, vests, shawls,

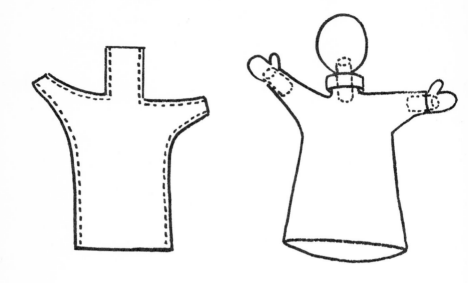

FIG. 24

or capes. A tie-on vest or separate skirt will give the best effect of a change of costume. Omit small fussy details that cannot be seen from a distance.

The characteristically short arms of a hand puppet can be lengthened by glueing cardboard tubes inside the sleeves (see Fig. 24). Pieces of plastic detergent bottles rolled into tube form and secured with an adhesive tape can also be used. Avoid lengthening the arms too much. Stiff arms are difficult to manipulate. Since the arm that is operated by the thumb is shorter than the other arm, a tube may be inserted into the shorter arm only.

The finger tubes must fit the finger snugly to pre-

vent the embarrassment caused by having it drop off
during a performance. Some puppeteers prefer to make
a tube that fits loosely in order to line it with thin plastic-
foam sheeting.

There are various kinds of puppet hands. Rigid hands
can be made of wood, papier maché, or sawdust mixture; the flexible ones can be made of felt, kid, or
chamois. Wire or pipe cleaner can be covered with any
of these materials, or bits of pipe cleaner can be shoved
up into the fingers after stitching. Felt hands are easiest
to make and most effective for hand puppets (Fig. 25).

Hands can be either mitten or glove-shape. Fingers
can be indicated on mittens and gloves by back-stitch-
ing lines. Glove fingers can be shaped at the tips (Fig.
26).

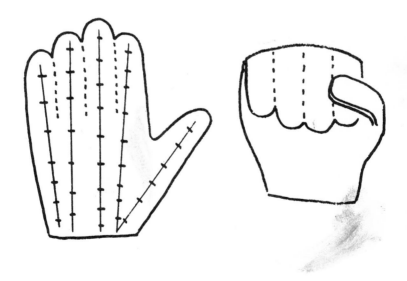

FIG. 25

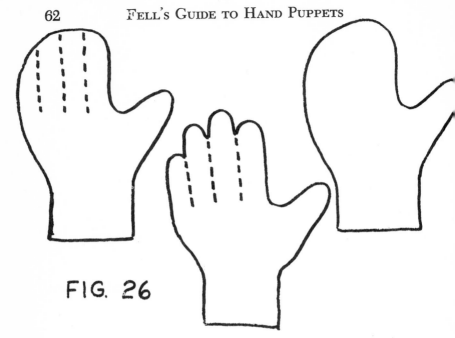

FIG. 26

Hands can pick up and carry small metal objects if a magnet is sewn into the palm.

The finished hand is sewn to the inside of the hemmed sleeve opening after which the finger tube is glued into the sleeve.

A hand puppet can be carried a step farther by giving it legs, but in general they can be very effective without them, since legs dangle out of control. They are most useful on puppets that must sit. When legs are added the operator's arm must be concealed by a black sleeve if the background is black; otherwise, use a color that will blend in with the background.

Simple legs can be made by cutting a piece of cloth as shown in Figure 27. Fold on the dotted line and stitch down the front of the leg. Turn inside out and

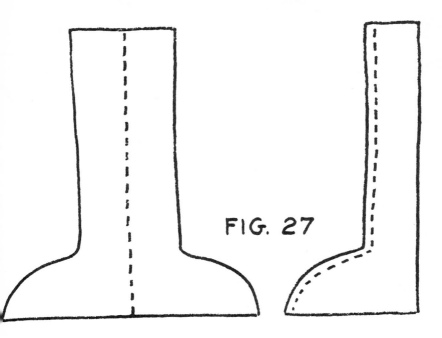

FIG. 27

sew across the bottom of the foot. Stuff it up to the knee and sew to make a joint. Stuff the upper leg and sew shut. Attach the legs to the under side of the costume at the waistline. Shorter legs without a joint can be attached to the under side of the hem.

For a more realistic leg and foot, the leg is shaped and the foot is given a sole. Make a leg pattern (Fig. 28), allowing ⅜-inch seams down the front and back of the leg and bottom of the foot. Allow ½-inch at the top of the leg. On a double piece of flesh-colored cloth, trace and cut out two sets of legs. Sew front and back seams and turn inside out. Hem the bottom of the foot.

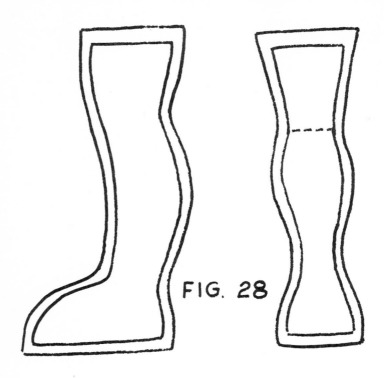

FIG. 28

Stand the leg upright on a piece of heavy cardboard and trace around the foot. This is the sole (Fig. 29-A). It must fit loosely inside the open foot. Sew a metal washer to the sole to give weight to the legs.

Trace around the cardboard sole on a piece of flesh-colored material. Allow ⅜-inches around the outside (Fig. 29-B). Cut out and sew around the outer edge. Place the cardboard sole in the center of the cloth, washer side up. Draw the thread tight around the sole. Pin the cloth-covered sole in place in the foot opening

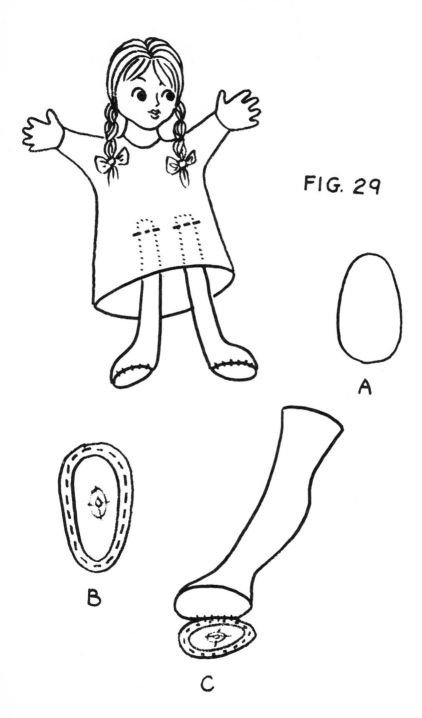

FIG. 29

A

B

C

FIG. 30

and overcast the sole of the foot (Fig. 29-C). Stuff the leg as described.

In Figure 30 the legs are sewn inside the skirt; the front and back of the skirt are sewn together and then sewn to the underside of the blouse front. The puppeteer slips his hand up under the back of the blouse, bypassing the skirt.

Instead of separate legs, a pants pattern with legs attached can be made (Fig. 31).

FIG. 31

To make felt shoes (Fig. 32), trace around the sole of the foot allowing ⅛-inch for a seam. Cut out a felt sole. Cut a piece of felt long enough to go around the outer edge of the sole and lap over ¼-inch (Fig. 32-A). It must be wide enough to come up over the front of the foot to the ankle. Overcast the strip of felt to the sole starting at the middle of the back. Slip the shoe onto the puppet's foot and tack the back of the shoe together. Starting at the back, cut the shoe top the desired height leaving an uncut section 2 inches wide at the front (Fig. 32-B). Bend the front felt down onto the instep and pin in place. Cut away the surplus felt, leav-

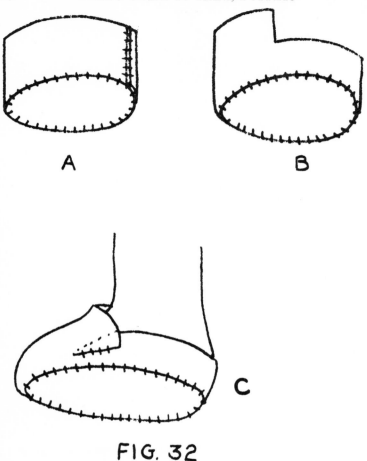

FIG. 32

ing a tongue which is tacked down to the sides at the darts (Fig. 32-C).

Dressing the erect walking animal puppet is the same as dressing people puppets except that paws or hooves replace hands (see Fig. 9). Animals that walk on all fours need bodies cut in two pieces (see Fig. 10). Allow plenty of room in the front legs for fingers. If the

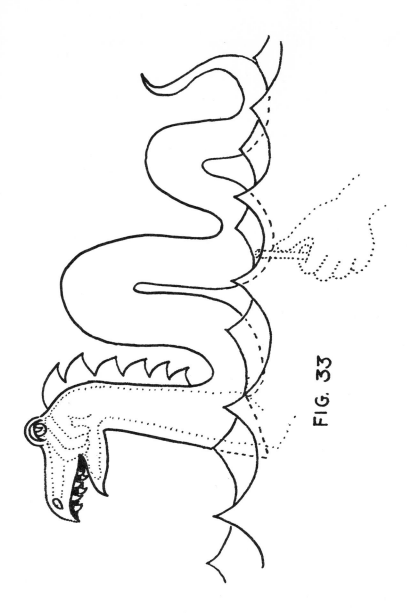

FIG. 33

animal has long legs, stuff the paws lightly and glue in finger tubes. The finger must reach the stuffing. The back legs should be stuffed lightly and tacked to the sleeve that disguises the puppeteer's arm. The body of an animal in a horizontal position can be propelled forward by a stick held in the free hand of the operator (Fig. 33).

Hooves can be made three-dimensional as are the human type feet (Fig. 34). Black felt hooves are effective on light-colored animals. Scallop the paws to indicate toes and sew or glue on pads of a contrasting color to the underside of each paw.

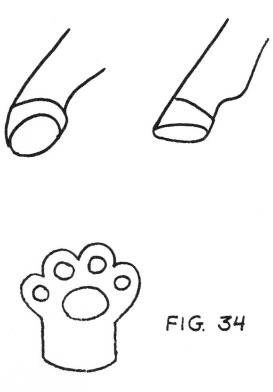

FIG. 34

Animal bodies can be permanently attached to the heads or can be removable.

The bodies of some animals present more of a challenge than others. The turtle shell is one of these (Fig. 35). A shell can be made of six layers of newspaper with wallpaper paste in between. While wet, make two shells by tracing around a 10-inch plate. Cut out the shells. From one shell cut out rounded portions on opposite sides through which the puppeteer's arm will slip (Fig. 35-A). Place hind legs and a tail made of stuffed felt between the shells before stapling them together. Place on a flat surface bottom side down and stuff the inside gently with crumpled newspaper until the upper shell is the desired length. When dry, remove the stuffing and reinforce the outer edge and underside openings with narrow strips of newspaper dipped in wallpaper paste.

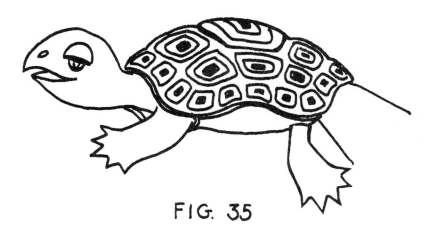

FIG. 35

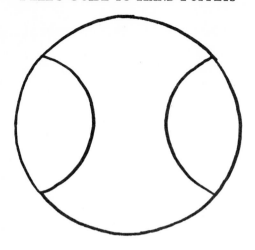

FIG. 35A

Another type of body that allows for more action is made of quilted cloth. Dark green with 2-inch squares is a good background for an effective and colorful design of felt, either glued or sewn on. An under shell of canvas or other heavy material is sewn to the upper shell using bias binding as a finish. By this method effective bugs can be made with many legs attached. The legs can be worked by the puppeteer's little finger, to which strings from the legs are attached.

Bodies can be made of a variety of materials—cloth, fur, imitation fur, or soft plastic. Plush, velvet, turkish toweling, and knitted fabrics are especially useful.

Furs with soft pliable skins are good. But do not use a fur with hair so long it obscures the animal shape.

Imitation fur, because it is more pliable than genuine fur, is easier to work with. It comes in many varieties —leopard, caracul, and Persian lamb; also, short and long haired, white, brown, tan, and black. Then there are the printed cloth patterns that imitate zebra, leopard, tiger, and ocelot, among others.

Chapter 7

The Stage

The hand-puppet stage can be improvised, built, or bought. It can be simple or complex depending upon the production and whether it will be permanently located or portable.

A puppet stage for children can be as uncomplicated as a broomstick draped with a sheet and tied between two chairs. It can be a table turned on its side or a partially boarded-up doorway.

Another impromptu children's stage is made by cutting the top from a large cardboard carton, inverting it and resting the sides on the edges of two card tables. Cut an opening on the front. Tape the sides of the box to the tables. A bed sheet or length of wrapping paper can be taped across the front to hide the puppeteers (Fig. 36).

The simplest permanent stage is a threefold hinged screen with a rectangular opening cut in the center section. The screen stands with the outer panels at right angles to the center panel. They are kept in place by a horizontal drop bar that fits into a slot and is held in place by a hook and eye or pin (Fig. 37).

This stage can be made of two sheets of 4 foot by 8

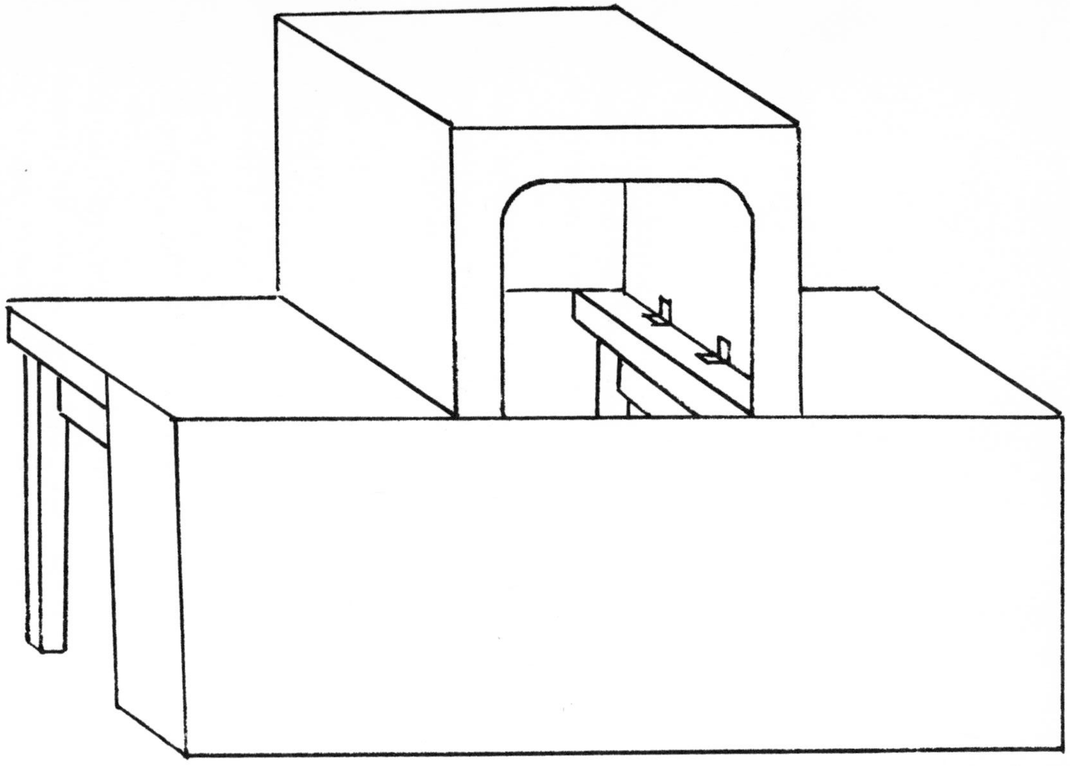

FIG. 36

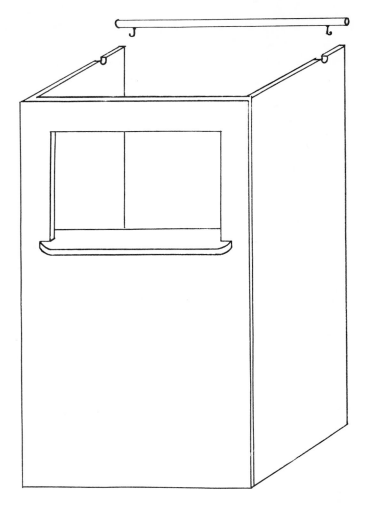

FIG. 37

foot plywood. If you use ¼-inch plywood, the stage can be stabilized with a 1 inch by 2 inch framework put together with mortise and tendon or half-lap joints, and glued and strengthened with plywood or metal corner brackets. Plywood ½-inch thick needs no stabilizing, but it is very heavy.

One sheet of plywood forms the center section; the second sheet cut in two lengthwise makes 2 foot by 8 foot side panels.

One foot or more can be cut from the height of this stage to cut down on weight. If it is set up in a permanent location, the weight and stability are assets.

The height of the opening, or proscenium, depends upon whether the stage is to be used by children or adults and whether they will sit or stand. For adults who will sit on movable stools, the stage can be approximately 4 feet from the bottom of the floor.

It is generally agreed that the best operating position is standing with arms outstretched. Since the stage height cannot be adjusted to each player, an average should be determined. This means the tallest operators must bend down or throw back their heads while the shorter members of the cast will stand on a narrow bench.

Some hand-puppet operators prefer a height of stage that will allow them to operate at chest level with a black semitransparent curtain between them and the audience (Fig. 38). The operator will not be seen if the lights are stronger in front of the curtain than behind it. There are many weaves of cloth that are semitransparent. Voile, some lining materials, sheer crepe, and

Woods Scene (see page 107).

Pond Scene (see pp. 106-107).

Scenes from "The Hunting Hoax" (pp. 156-157).

Stage set for "The Bear and the Honey Bucket" (pp. 172-173).

Early steps in modeling the puppet head.

Painting the puppet head.

Painted head drying in soda bottle.

Attaching hair to a painted head.

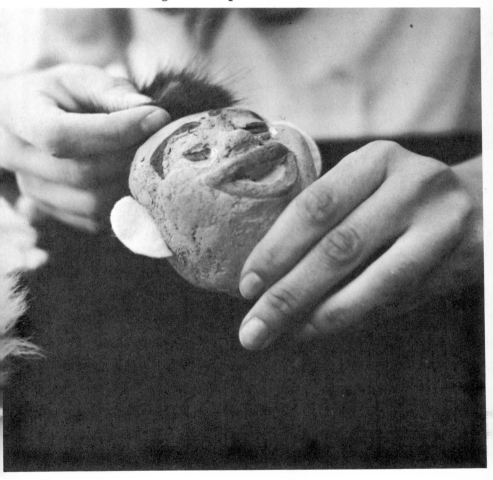

"Human" puppets on stage with three-dimensional backdrop.

Hand position in finished head before costume is attached.

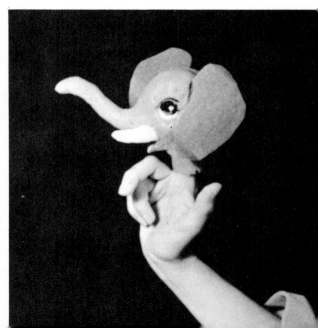

FIG. 38

even a cheap grade of velveteen will allow sufficient vision. The arm covered with a black sleeve extends from under the curtain to operate the puppet. The stage floor will be between 4 feet and 4½-feet.

This arrangement has the advantage of allowing the

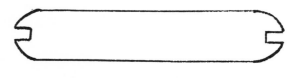

FIG. 39

FIG. 40

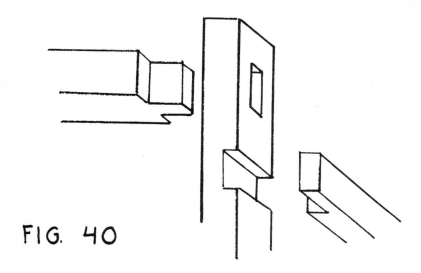

FIG. 40

puppeteer to observe the puppets' movements and the disadvantage of restricting his mobility. It also eliminates the need for a scenic backdrop.

After cutting the stage opening, make the stage floor or playboard (Fig. 39). It should be no wider than 5 inches. A rectangular board 2 inches longer than the stage opening is notched in the ends to fit around the sides of the opening. All corners should be rounded. A removable playboard will allow for stage folding. Use a hook and eye to hold it in place.

Another type of three-part screen is made of a framework of ¾-inch by 1⅝-inch standard cut pine put together with mortise and tendon or half-lap joints (Fig. 40), glued together, and strengthened at the corners with metal or wood angle brackets. The stage sections are covered with canvas or other stiff cloth hemmed at the bottom. Wood or iron rods are slipped into the hems to keep the curtains in place. A 54-inch by 80-inch front with 24-inch wings should meet most needs.

A more elaborate curtain covering for the framework can be made by box-pleating sailcloth or corduroy which is attached to the framework with snap-on tape. The receiving part of the tape can be nailed on or glued on with epoxy glue.

A collapsible stage that folds into three compact pieces for easy carrying can be made of a framework of 1⅛-inch by 3⅝-inch standard cut pine (Fig. 41). Each section is hinged so that the top folds forward onto the bottom part. The sections are held in place by screen couplings that swivel on a screw to allow the sections to fold. Use two couplings to a section. The panels are held together by drawpin hinges, allowing separation of the panels. Box-pleated curtains attached with snap-on tape complete the stage.

Attach hinge pins with wire or strong cord to the framework, and keep extras of all attachments.

A walking stage on which the puppeteer can perform as he moves from room to room in a hospital or school is of simple construction (Fig. 41-A). Take a cardboard carton, cut a hole in the bottom large enough for the puppeteer to put his head through. Cut the same size hole in a piece of ¼-inch plywood that is large enough to protrude 3 or 4 inches from the front of the box. This forms the playboard. Cut away the box front and attach a piece of semitransparent black material. The puppeteer will be able to see through the curtain, enabling him to see where he is going, but he will not be

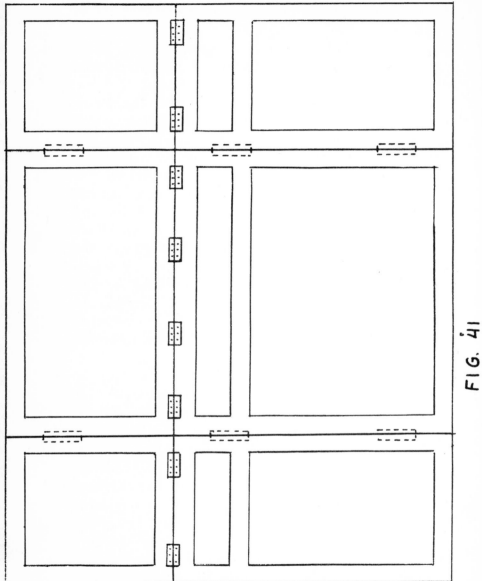

FIG. 41

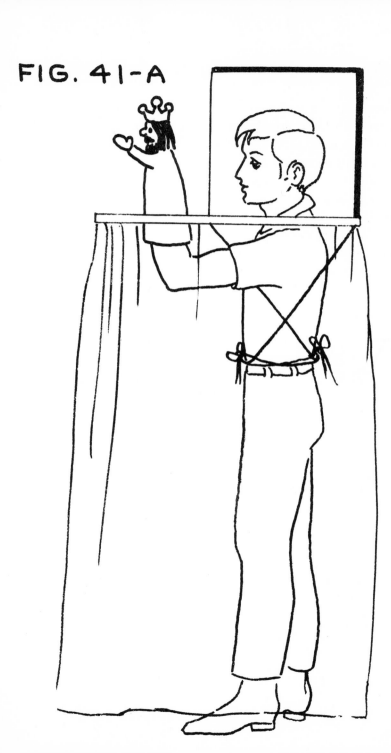

FIG. 41-A

seen. Attach cords to the four corners of the board underneath. The cords cross over on both front and back and are snapped to a wide belt that fits snugly around the puppeteer's waist. If the receiving part of snap tape is glued to the edge of the board and the snap part is sewed to a lightweight drapery, it can be easily removed for storage.

The stages described were planned for hand puppets exclusively. Combination stages can be made for the use of more than one kind of puppet.

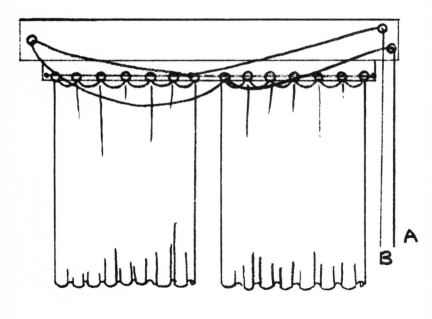

A
B

FIG. 42 DRAW CURTAIN

The Front Curtain

The stage curtain functions as a center of interest when it is closed. It also shuts the stage off while scenery is being changed, or it may be shut to denote the passage of time or to separate acts or scenes.

The choice of material will depend upon the mechanism used to close the curtain. There are several methods of stringing. Figure 42 shows a draw-type curtain. It is made of two parts and hangs from rings on a metal rod. Cord A opens the curtain, and B closes it. The ends

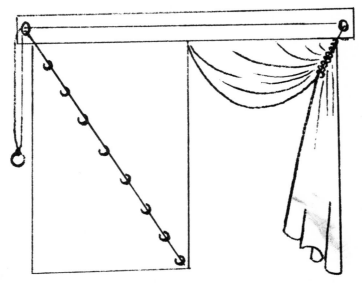

FIG. 43 DRAPED CURTAIN

can be knotted together or attached to a weight that
keeps them taut when the curtain is open. This curtain
can be made of any material that will hang in folds,
such as velvet, velveteen, or some of the soft synthetic
fabrics. Figure 43 shows a draped curtain. This also is
made in two parts. The upper edges are tacked to a
batten. Rings are sewn diagonally across each curtain.
The cord is strung as shown. Weights should be sewn
at the inside corner of each half. This curtain is less
used and generally less satisfactory. Figure 44 is a drop
curtain. The material is tacked to a batten. It should
not be as heavy as for either the draw or draped types.

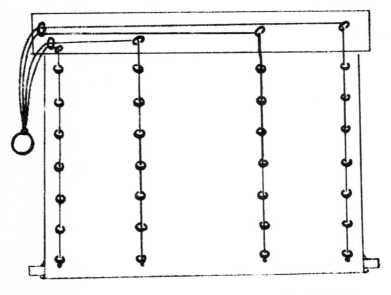

FIG 44 DROP CURTAIN

It must gather up softly. Cords are run through rings as shown. For ease of operation, tie the cords to a ring. Make sure that they all are the same length. Drapery weights or a dowel stick in the bottom hem will help to bring the curtain down.

All curtains should be light-proof.

Chapter 8.

Visibility, Scenery, and Properties

Visibility

To avoid playing to a frustrated audience, it is necessary to understand the problem of visibility, both vertical and horizontal.

Vertical visibility is an acute problem on the hand-puppet stage because the stage is always above the eye level of front-row spectators. The problem is even greater when the puppet stage is placed on a raised platform. From a study of Figure 45, one must conclude that, if possible, the stage should be placed on the same level as the front row seats; the puppets should act as close to the playboard as possible, and as they are moved back they must be raised slightly.

Horizontal visibility must also be calculated. The closer the spectator is to the center of the auditorium, the better he is able to see action on the stage. The most undesirable positions are the outer seats in the front row (Fig. 46). The triangle in the center of the stage is seen by the entire audience; the shaded portions will

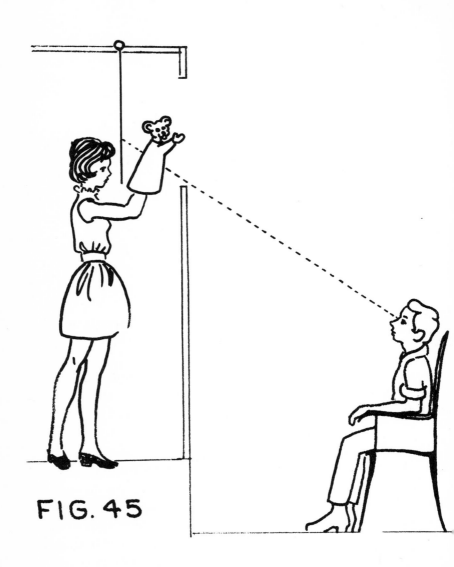

FIG. 45

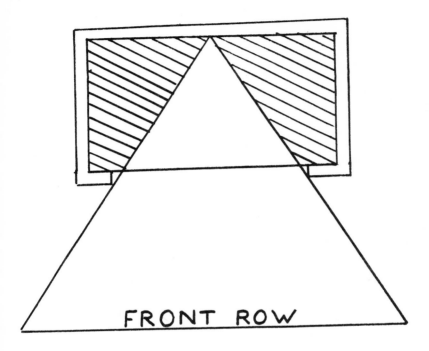

FIG. 46

be seen by a part of the audience. From this we recognize the necessity of placing important props and carrying on vital action in the center area.

Care must also be taken when placing the backdrop
that the upper edge is not seen by the front-row spectators and the lower edge by the spectators in the back
row. Decorative detail essential to the play, if it is to be
visible to most of the audience, must be painted in the
middle section neither too low nor too far to the sides.

Scenery

With these facts in mind we will get on with making and decorating a backdrop. The size depends upon the size of the back opening of the puppet theater. The drop should fill the space from side to side, and, as just mentioned, be so placed that no one can see over or under it.

Backdrops can be made in a number of ways and of many kinds of materials depending on how much use they will get.

A simple backdrop of heavy paper will last for some time if the paper is bent over 1 inch all around and glued down. On the top edge punch holes 1 inch in from either end, and one in the middle. Looseleaf reinforcements glued around the holes prevent tearing. In our art classes, string was pulled through the holes and tied in loops large enough to accommodate a ¾-inch pole. We were in possession of several wooden curtain rods which made it possible to ready all of our drops at one time. They were hung across the top of the puppet stage in order of their use. After a scene was used, it was moved to the rear, making the next scene available.

If you are going to work with one pole, screw three cup hooks at intervals into a ⅝-inch dowel stick that is long enough to extend 3 inches over the top edges of the puppet theater. Space the hooks in accordance with the holes in the backdrop. Use string loops; the drop will last longer and be easier to remove from the hooks.

Instead of paper, our classes used cardboard. We were fortunate in having large sheets of corrugated cardboard with a good grade of white paper on one side. They were discards from a paper box factory. Such windfalls are possible in any community. We were also given scrap felt and quantities of styrofoam by kindly manufacturers.

Another type of backdrop works on the principle of the old-fashioned roller towel. Sew a length of muslin or windowshade material into a continuous band. Slip a dowel stick through the pole and hang it across the top of the puppet theater. Apply a thin sizing of gum arabic to muslin before applying paint. You can also use the muslin as a background upon which the painted scenes are pinned.

A backdrop can also be made by sewing several sheets of heavy paper or sized muslin bookwise across the top and attaching it to a dowel stick. A page can be flipped back over the rod to reveal the next scene.

For some plays a three-dimensional backdrop is desirable. It can be made by attaching houses, bridges or other structures to a heavy cardboard drop on which a scene has been painted. If the building is made large enough, a puppet can enter and exit through the door. Lightweight construction is necessary, such as a cardboard frame covered with paper, since it is attached by stapling or gluing.

Styrofoam can also be used when making a three-dimensional backdrop. Being lightweight, it is ideal. Among other things, it can be used to make pillars,

arches, steps, or buildings. This might be considered
for a dramatization needing a Greek or Roman background.

Backdrops can be done in layers or planes to give
depth (Fig. 47). The painted backdrop (A) is hung at
the back (B); the cut of trees hangs about 6 inches in
front of (A). With this arrangement a puppet can
emerge from behind the trees. If the cut-out has a
house among the trees, the puppet can go in and out
of the house. To prevent the cut-out from swaying, attach it to an angle iron screwed to the side of the puppet
theater. If it is not necessary that the puppet emerge
from behind the trees, a foreground can be attached
(C).

If you are working with children it may be necessary
to set a limit on the number of scenes in their play. Their
enthusiasm runs high at this point. Caution them that
constant changing of scenes slows down the action and
can be extremely distracting. Impress upon them the
necessity of keeping the design simple. It must be understood at a glance and make immediate impact even
to the spectators in the back row. This will eliminate
fussy detail.

I find it a good idea to have many 9 by 12 or 12 by
18 sketches made of the proposed scene. They can be
individual work or the combined work of several stu-
dents. When the drawing to be used is chosen, divide
it into squares. Divide the backdrop into the same
number of squares. By this method an accurate copy of
the original can be made.

The same advice given in Chapter 3 on painting

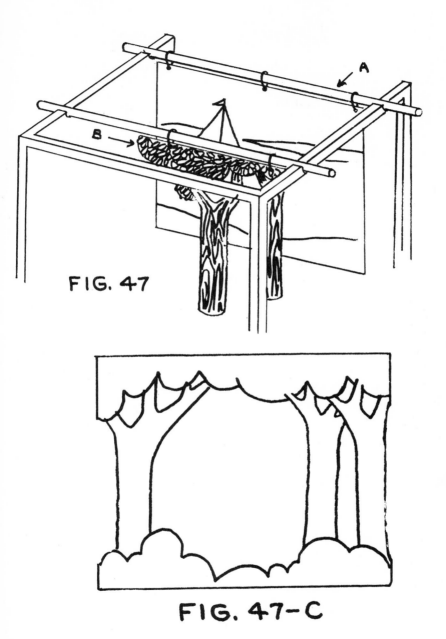

FIG. 47

FIG. 47-C

heads applies to painting backdrops. Watercolors, crayons, tempera, oils, or acrylics can be used. I favor tempera because most schools have it on hand. It is fast-drying, mistakes can be painted over, and it can be waterproofed with a fixative spray.

For special effects, luminous or fluorescent paints or paper can be used.

Simple plays can be performed in front of an unobtrusive sky backdrop of fluffy clouds, a stormy sky, or a sunset.

Effective backdrops can be made of cut paper pasted on the backdrop. This method need not be limited to children. A fanciful design, if not overpowering, makes an interesting background, especially when colored lights are played on it.

From time to time, as you are working, place the puppets to be used in front of the backdrop and turn on the lights. Study the effect. Color tends to wash out under strong artificial light. If this happens you will have to make the scene brighter or darker. The scene may appear spotty with some areas jumping out at you. They will need toning down. If the puppets do not stand out against the background, it may be because you used the same colors for the background and the costumes or both are dark or light. In the woods scene (see photo section), the puppets were overpowered by the intensity of the red-brown trees. When they were grayed and lightened by a wash of blue mixed with white, the backdrop assumed its proper background role.

The opposite was the case with the pond scene with the two ducks (see photo section). The white duck did not show up against the light blue pond but stood out beautifully when the water was darkened.

These corrections saved us the embarrassment of discovering our mistakes along with the audience.

Properties

Only the properties that are essential to the play should be used. They must assist the play, not hide it. Storing them backstage between acts can be a problem. I recall the dilemma of two seventh-grade boys whose gallon can containing pebbles tipped over and rolled noisily toward the audience.

If possible, props should be placed on the playboard in such a manner as not to obstruct the view of the audience or restrict the action of the puppets.

Bushes, fences, stumps, or flowers must be kept low, trees thin and tall (Fig. 48). A tree branch anchored in a base of plastacine can be used if branches that might catch on puppet clothing are pruned. Blossoms or leaves of crepe or tissue paper can be pasted to the limbs. Plastic flowers, if they are in proportion to the puppets, are effective in front of a picket fence made of cardboard.

Books on creative paper design show ways of constructing decorative trees, flowers, and other useful props (see Bibliography).

Because hand puppets generally behave boisterously, props should be anchored to prevent tipping. When possible, they should be weighted from within with stones or attached to the playboard with an adhesive tape. They can also be weighted on the bottom with a

FIG. 48

piece of lead. Cardboard tables and chairs can be thumbtacked to the playboard if a small piece of cardboard is bent at right angles and glued or stapled to the inside of the leg.

There are various other ways of attaching props to the playboard. They can be fastened to ¼-inch dowel sticks and plugged into holes drilled in the playboard.

Depth can be achieved by extending the prop back from the playboard. Drill a ⅛-inch bolt hole 1-inch from the end of a ¼-inch by 1-inch by 5-inch slat. Drill a corresponding hole in the playboard 1-inch in from the back edge. In the other end of the slat, drill a hole for a ¼″ dowel stick to which the prop is attached. Fasten the slat to the underside of the playboard with a bolt and wing nut (see Fig. 48). When not in use the prop can be removed, the wing nut loosened, and the slat swung beneath the playboard.

Another method is to saw slots at intervals into the back edge of the playboard. Cut a piece of tin the length and thickness of the playboard. Shape the tin to the rounded corners and nail down. Into the slots thus formed, slip paddles on which props are nailed.

Arches and columns as part of a three-dimensional backdrop were previously discussed. They can also be used to good advantage on the playboard.

The arch can be formed around the stage opening with columns on either side. It can be a two-dimensional drawing or painting on cardboard, or a three-dimensional cardboard or styrofoam setup. The arch must not be too thick; 1 inch will give a feeling of depth.

Columns can be made of styrofoam or of corrugated cardboard which makes excellent fluted pillars when rolled into cylinders. Combined with styrofoam blocks at top and bottom they are very convincing.

Corrugated cardboard is also useful in making roofs. It comes in a variety of colors.

Occasionally a prop is too large to fit on the playboard. Such props, usually a bed or table, can stand in the space between the backdrop and playboard if attached to a wooden framework (Fig. 49). The drawback is that it limits the space in which the puppeteers move about.

This brings us to the subject of furniture. The most commonly used pieces are beds, tables and chairs. Doll

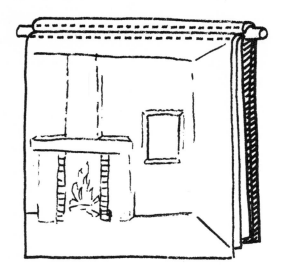

FIG. 49

furniture that is in scale with the puppets can be used and may be found in dime stores along with other useful props.

However, almost any piece of furniture can be made from boxes or cartons. Oatmeal boxes, salt boxes, and cheese cartons become round tables. Square tables are made from milk cartons. With a little effort a flat Kleenex, candy or stocking box can be made into a bed; a tall, slender box makes a grandfather's clock. Children enjoy making furniture.

In making a table, decide first on the height, then cut off the excess. The legs can be equally spaced on a round table by finding the center of the top. Draw two equidistant lines through the center, extending them down the sides of the box to position the legs (Fig. 50-A).

Square tables are easier; the legs are cut at the corners.

Cheese carton tables (Fig. 50-B) must have an extra top glued on to cover the indentation. The tablecloth should also be glued in place as should dishes, pots, and pans, which can be made of clay and painted when dry.

But, again, go easy on the props; they will be distracting if they are overdone.

The simplest form of chair can be made from a milk carton cut down to seat height (Fig. 50-C). Make a back of heavy cardboard that is as wide as the chair and extends from the bottom of the carton to the desired height for a back. Chair backs can be solid, spindled, or any style you wish. If a throne is needed, make an extra large chair with a high ornate back and place it on a low box dais. Backs and chair seats can be stapled together.

Any rectangular box that is not too thick can become a bed by gluing or stapling on a headboard and footboard of heavy cardboard (Fig. 50-D). For added strength, glue pieces of cardboard bent at right angles to the underside of the bed at the joining of the bed and its parts. Add a pillow and a gay patchwork quilt.

To prevent paint from crawling when painting over the plastic coating on milk cartons, add a few drops of liquid detergent to tempera paints.

Props that are attached to sticks can be moved from below the stage. But, be careful that you do not have a

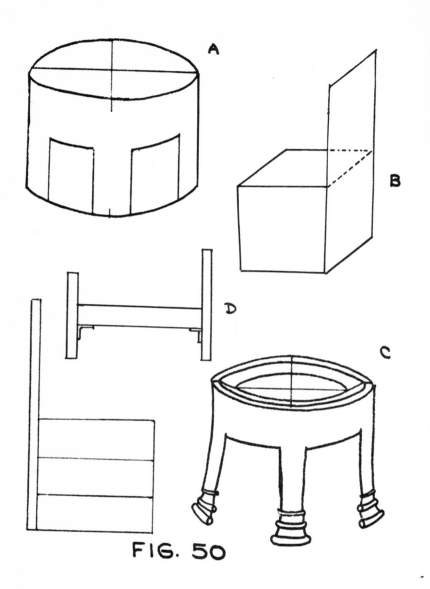

FIG. 50

traffic mixup. Practice in order to find the best way of handling the situation. In a skit put on by an eighth-grade class, two puppets stood on a street corner conversing while cars passed back and forth on the street behind them. Cars from advertising circulars were pasted on heavy cardboard and cut out. One boy handled all the cars. Tooting horns added realism to the scene. The painting on the backdrop was an extension of the street.

Props can be made to move upward by attaching a string to the top of a rocket, plane, bird, or butterfly. Pass the string over a pole that rests across the top of the puppet theater. By pulling down on the string, the prop will move upward. It may be necessary to attach a string to the bottom of the prop to prevent it from spinning or swaying. One operator can control both strings.

Three-dimensional butterflies and birds are within the capabilities of children in the lower elementary grades. Rockets and planes can be made by the upper-grade pupils.

Because it is such a fun thing, I suggest the making of a hollow stump. Bunnies, chipmunks, skunks, any small animal can pop up from within the stump to the delight of the children.

The stump must be attached to the back edge of the playboard so that the operator can thrust his arm up through the hollow stump.

Make the stump by modeling papier maché on wallpaper paste and sawdust mixture over a cardboard ring. Make sure it is large enough for a hand to pass through

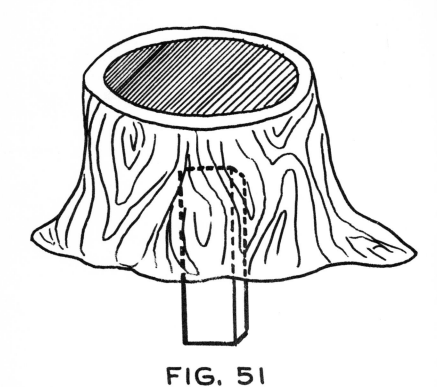

FIG. 51

with ease. Build the mixture out at the bottom to show the beginning of the large roots (Fig. 51).

Small animals can also look out of holes in three trunks painted on the backdrop.

For a humorous note, the animal could wear eyeglasses made of bent pipe cleaner. An owl would look very learned wearing glasses.

There are no end of props that can be made or purchased. A duck could carry an umbrella from the dime store where many useful props, such as guns, swords, drums, and pianos, can be found. Hang a drum around the neck of an animal and have him beat time to the marching of a parade of strange characters. Write a story around the incident.

Chapter 9.

Puppet Action and
the Puppet Voice

No matter how well made the puppet or how good the play, props, and scenery, you can still give a boring performance if your puppet doesn't come alive through its movements. The puppet is your tool and will do the things you make it do.

To learn the possibilities and limitations of your puppet, practice in front of a mirror. The very first thing you must learn is to keep the puppet at a constant height. Heights should also relate to one another. An adult is taller than a child. An adult who starts out taller than the other puppets in a play must remain so. As a puppet moves back from the playboard he must be raised slightly. Try to keep him within 6 to 8 inches of the playboard. Never raise the puppet so that your arm is exposed.

When you have mastered these basic problems of manipulation, you are free to concentrate upon the many things your puppet can do.

Begin with simple movements. Face the mirror with

your puppet on your hand. Slowly turn your wrist so the puppet is in profile. Make him look up, then down. Practice walking. Keep your arm upright; the tendency is to allow him to lean forward at an unnatural angle. Be sure he is not listing toward one side.

A puppet reveals its personality through its walk. Try the walk of an old person bent over, shifting weight slowly from one side to the other, with his head nodding slightly as he plods along. Now try the fast confident walk of a younger person, the skipping joyous walk of a child. By sweeping arm movements puppets can move very rapidly.

Inexperienced hand-puppet operators tend to keep their puppet's arms waving in the air constantly for no reason and to jiggle the puppet aimlessly.

Now, explore the capabilities of your little actor. The thing that he can do better than any other type of puppet is pick up objects. If his hands are supple, and they will be if they are made of felt, you can shove the tips of your fingers down into his hands. Bend down, bring the hands together around an object, straighten up, carry it away and set it down.

If pieces of pipe cleaner are sewed into the insides of his palms, his hands can be wrapped around objects. He can carry a club, fishpole, or broom, but he must be taken off stage to have it removed.

He can even pick up small metal objects if a magnet has been sewed into his palm.

Hands can be very expressive. By putting both palms to his face the puppet can express consternation; with one palm to his face he is thinking; with palms over his ears, he is shutting out unwanted sounds.

He can shut doors, wash windows, turn a wheel if his hand is attached to the wheel, wash his face, point, or sweep if the broom is attached to his hand. He is known for his ability to use a club. He can lift and shove furniture. These motions are conveyed by the body as well as the hands. Your wrist is the puppet's waist.

Let us examine the movements that take place when a puppet scrubs a floor (Fig. 52). Bend your wrist forward until the puppet appears to be on its knees. Rest the hand on the little finger and next finger closed tightly against the palm. Bring the thumb and third finger which operate the puppet's arms down to the floor. The puppet can scrub with either hand. Use the one

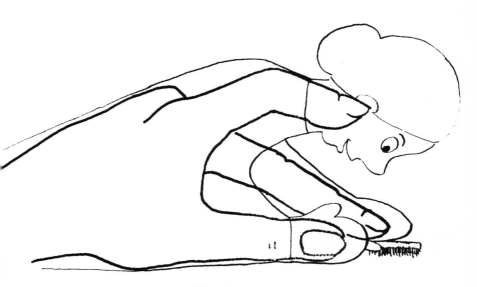

FIG. 52

which you can rotate most easily. With a small brush tied to its hand, it will scrub most convincingly.

A puppet can nod his head up and down in agreement, but to turn his head back and forth for a "no" gesture, the whole body turns.

Try practicing with a puppet on either hand or with another person and his puppet. Have the puppets bow low, shake hands, embrace, chase one another, hand objects back and forth, and do exercises together. Have your puppets sit down and talk with nods and gestures. When puppets are talking, keep in mind an old puppet rule which says that the puppet who is speaking should be in movement. A gesture of the hand or a slight movement of the head is enough to identify him as the speaker if the other puppets remain motionless while he is speaking.

Have your puppets dance together. It is difficult to convey formal dance movements because of the lack of legs, but plausible rendition of a modern dance, with its gyrations, gestures, bending, and turning, is fairly easy. Have the puppets dance together and separately; whirl around, bend back, then forward, and touch hands. The challenge of portraying young people dancing will appeal especially to the upper-grade pupils.

The Puppet Voice

When you have gained mechanical control of your puppet, establish its manner of speaking. Characters must be distinct from one another; the voice helps to make the distinction. Choose a voice that agrees with the physical appearance of the puppet.

Give a small, gentle animal a babyish, high-pitched voice; give a large and fierce beast a heavy deep snarling voice. An old man might speak with a quavery delivery, a fairy princess with a sweet, thin voice; a slow, heavy hesitating voice would suit a stupid fellow, and a nasal cackle belongs to a wicked witch.

There are many ways of changing your voice. The old puppetmasters altered their voices by putting a form of whistle in their mouths. The voice can be pitched at different levels. Whatever manner of speaking you choose, be sure that you can be easily understood. A squeaky voice pitched so high that you cannot maintain it throughout a performance would be a poor choice. Never strain your voice.

Speaking into a tin can, holding your nose while speaking, or speaking with an accent are a few of many possible voice changes.

Speaking with an accent will require study. Perhaps you know someone with an ethnic accent; if not, TV offers a number of regulars who portray Germans, Mexicans, Indians, among others.

When a narrator is needed to read descriptive or narrative passages between scenes or acts of a play, choose a person who enunciates clearly and speaks slowly. The most frequent faults of the amateur speaker are speaking too fast, letting the voice drop so that it is inaudible at the end of a sentence, and slurring words. Recording voices on a tape recorder and then playing them back is an excellent way of correcting faulty speech. The usual response is, "Do I sound like *that?*" After some practice, tape again; the improvement will be astonishing.

Hand-puppet performances should not be given to a very large audience because the size of the puppets and the fact that the puppeteers' voices usually come from below stage and are muffled, but this cannot always be avoided. On several occasions our puppet plays were given in the gymnasium which also serves as an auditorium. Though the audience was small, and the chairs placed close to the stage, the children could not be heard. We solved the problem by using the public address system; most schools have one. The microphone was hung on a hook on the inside front of the stage out of the way of the children, thus avoiding the annoying crackling sounds that would have resulted from continual handling and bumping of the "mike."

Chapter 10

Lights, Music, and Special Sound Effects

Lights give an authentic theater touch to a puppet show in addition to creating mood and changes in the weather and the time of day.

A very simple lighting arrangement for a children's show consists of a floor lamp set up where it will cast light on the stage opening.

Equally simple is a stage placed below a ceiling light from which a cord is dropped. Enclose the bulb in a wire cage to keep it from coming in contact with people or fabric.

A more elaborate setup consists of gooseneck lamps attached to the front or sides of the stage opening, directing the light onto the puppets. Lamps with slots on the undersides of the bases can be hooked onto the stage and easily removed when not in use (Fig. 53).

Make sure that spectators sitting at the ends of the first row will not be looking straight into a light.

Photographers' floodlights with clamps are attached to the inside of the side panels to light the backdrop.

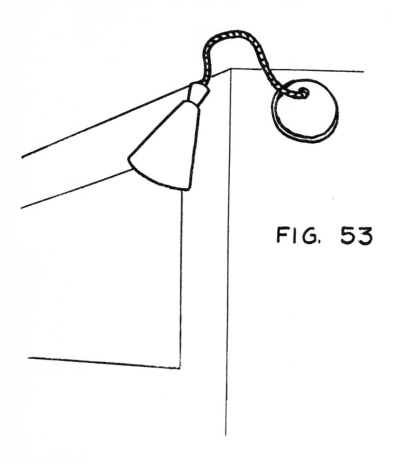

FIG. 53

In place of gooseneck lamps, bulbs in sockets, mounted on strips of wood, can be cantilevered from above the proscenium on either side. For this arrangement, reflectors are needed. You can buy them or make simple, durable ones from aluminum pie plates (Fig. 54). Cut away the pie plate rim, leaving a 6½-inch circle. Find the center and with a compass draw a circle with

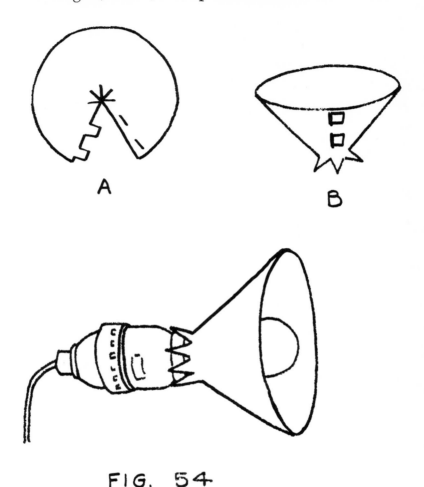

FIG. 54

a 1½-inch diameter. Draw a wedge shape using the center point as an axis and a base of 3 inches on the rim edge. Draw tabs ½-inch square and slits into which the tabs will fit, as shown. Cut out the wedge, leaving the tabs. With a pointed knife or razor blade, cut the slits. Make eight cuts from the center of the disk to the 1½-inch diameter line. Slip the tabs into slots, bend the center points outward, and fit the reflector over the empty light socket. The points will hold it in place.

There are single- and double-socket swivel-head holders on the market that make excellent front stage fixtures if they are provided with reflectors.

For special effects use a 35 mm. slide projector. Color can be obtained by fitting colored gelatine, the professional kind that is fireproof, into 35 mm. slide frames from a camera shop. Set up the projector in the back of the room.

A spotlight or two can be used as "follow" lights and can be placed in the back and to the sides.

Always keep a flashlight backstage for emergencies.

Colored lights can do much to enhance a puppet production if properly used. Color can set the mood. Pink, yellow, and orange suggest gayety, good cheer, and comedy. Dark, cool, somber colors suggest a sinister depressing atmosphere. When planning special effects, care should be taken to provide sufficient light to be able to see the puppets clearly.

Colors can do strange things to puppets. Green light gives a ghastly look to skin color. There are times when this is the effect you want. Under blue-green light, red appears black. Red cheeks will look like ugly black smudges. Pink light is as kind to puppets as it is to humans. It makes them come alive with a rosy glow.

Music

Music is essential to a puppet production. It fills in while the audience is being seated and while they are leaving. It can accompany a song, dance, or pantomime or can be used between acts.

Overture music sets the mood; it suggests what is to come. Music can be soft and romantic, fiery and intense, lilting, gay, or rollicking. Since the logical actions of a hand puppet are slapstick comedy, the music to fit their usual performance would have a gay vitality with a marked rhythm—folk songs, dance music.

Music should be simple, not overpowering. A piano or phonograph will supply the type of music needed. Most schools have a fair selection of recordings in their music departments.

The operator of the phonograph has the responsibility of keeping the volume under control and of playing the right music at the right moment. It is difficult to put the needle down at the proper place without marking the spot with a piece of masking tape. Keep a flashlight handy for this exacting job. Be sure the records are marked as to when they are played and have them stacked in the order of their playing. Be alert for the stage manager's cue.

Do not play overture music too long. It should be played after the house lights are out and lights on the front of the stage are on. The music should stop when the curtain goes up. Follow the same procedure before each act.

Special Sound Effects

A puppet play will profit by special sound effects if they are not overdone. A great variety of effects are possible with simple devices. The clopping of horse's hooves can be imitated by pounding two plastic bowls, face down on a table; thunder, by shaking a sheet of galvanized tin or by rolling BB shot on a drumhead; thunder can be accompanied by lightning if a jagged opening is cut in the backdrop and a light is flashed back of the cut. It can also be simulated with a photographer's flash. BB shot dropped on a drumhead produces the sound of rain; the sound of breaking glass can be made by pouring broken glass into a metal can; shots are made with blank cartridges when used in an auditorium or with a cap pistol in a smaller room. An explosion is produced by popping a paper bag or slapping a board against the floor; smoke is produced by burning punk, rope, or cigarettes. Keep water backstage to "shut off" the smoke.

Special effects can be recorded on a tape recorder. This is something children can do and enjoy. The farm, zoo, and railroad station are good locations for special sounds.

Phonograph records are available with special sound effects. There are records with sounds of one kind, such as train noises, and others that have a great variety of sounds. See the Sources for Supplies section for record companies that handle such records.

A tiny music box with its tinkly music comes in handy for fairy scenes.

Novelty, dime stores, and music stores have whistles that produce mooing, barking, mewing, and chirping sounds. There are also "talking" books that produce animal sounds, but there is nothing wrong with the children themselves doing the sounds.

Parts or themes of the following music is suggested for use with various types of puppet productions:

General

Carnival of Animals	Saint-Saëns
Golliwogs Cake Walk	Debussy
Mother Goose Suite	Ravel
Surprise Symphony	Haydn
Waltzes	Brahms
Chopsticks	Folk Tune
Amaryllis	Folk Tune
76 Trombones	Wilson
Flight of the Bumble Bee	Rimsky-Korsakov
Hary Janos	Kodaly
Syncopated Clock	Anderson
March of the Toys	Herbert
The Doll Dance	Poldine
Parade of the Wooden Soldiers	Jessel
Peter and the Wolf	Prokofiev
Pieces Faciles	Stravinsky

Horror

Danse Macabre ....Saint-Saëns
Night on Bald Mountain ....Moussorgsky
The Hall of the Mountain King ....Grieg
Cinderella Suite ....Prokofiev
Sorcerer's Apprentice ....Dukas

Western

The Grand Canyon Suite ....Grofe
Billy the Kid Suite ....Copeland
Rodeo ....Copeland

March

March Militaire ....Schubert

Chapter 11.

The Production

The production of a puppet show involves planning and organizing. The bigger the production, the more work is necessary. Whatever the size, the number of people involved in producing the play should be kept to a minimum to avoid confusion.

For a well-coordinated performance, there should be a house manager and stage manager with workers who are in charge of lights, sound, special effects, music, and tape recorder. Depending upon the size and type of organization, there may be a need for an advertising manager, business manager, and publicity man.

The house manager is in charge of the room or auditorium and the ushers. It is his duty to cue the stage manager when the last person is seated and the audience is ready for the performance. The stage manager then takes over. He directs the above-mentioned workers.

How the room is set up depends upon its size and shape and the size of the audience. Figure 55 shows a possible setup. The puppet theater stands at one end of the room with enough space between it and the rear wall for puppeteers to enter and exit from the theater.

Somewhere in this area an emergency kit should be

FIG. 55

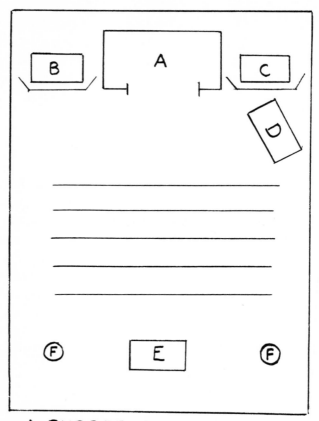

A. PUPPET STAGE
B. SPECIAL SOUND EFFECTS
C. TAPE RECORDER, PHONOGRAPH
D. PIANO
E. PROJECTOR
F. SPOT LIGHTS

kept. This might be a box or basket in which extra extension cords, light bulbs, wire nails, glue, scissors, pliers, electrician's scotch tape, pins, and a hammer are kept.

Chairs for the audience are arranged in front of the stage, allowing, if possible, nine feet between the front row and the stage.

A well-padded special sound-effects table is placed behind a screen and to one side of the puppet theater. The sound-effects equipment and flashlight are laid out on the table in order of their use. The person in charge of this table should have a list of sounds and when they occur, and be on the alert for cues. There is little worse than a sound that comes after it is needed.

On the opposite side of the theater, behind another screen, a table holds a tape recorder, phonograph, and flashlight. If records furnish the music, they should be marked with the act and scene in which they are played. If they are not played from the beginning, a piece of tape should mark the spot where the needle is to be put down.

If a piano furnishes the music, it can replace the table that holds the recorder and phonograph. The piano should be in such a position that the pianist can see the stage. He should also have enough light by which to read his music. A pianist who can improvise and fill in if need be is a real asset. If music accompanies a dance, song, or pantomime, the playing time must be worked out carefully so that the puppet does not have to repeat the same words or motions over and over.

If a projector is used, it should be set up at the back

of the room. A chair placed on a table may be necessary to bring the lens on a level with the stage.

If the play is given in a classroom in the daytime, light from the windows must be blocked out; also, cover glass in doors leading to corridors. Most classrooms are equipped with lightproof draperies; if not, mask out the light with black paper.

If yours is a group giving a puppet play to raise money, it will be necessary to advertise your show. For this an advertising man is needed. If the show is to be put on only once or twice, notices in the local paper or papers, window cards in downtown stores and libraries, and radio and TV coverage on local stations will get the word around. You might also ask club presidents to announce the place and date of the production.

If you plan to put the show "on the road," your publicity man will have a bigger job. An advertising campaign must be planned. For a start, write to the chambers of commerce in nearby towns for lists of club presidents. These include men's and women's clubs, 4H and boy and girl scout clubs (if the play will be of interest to children), service institutions, schools, parent-teacher associations, and colleges. They are possible sponsors. Don't overlook hostesses who are giving large private parties. Department stores, especially during the Christmas season, might consider puppet pantomime shows in their windows or puppet shows in their toy departments.

Make sure the daily papers have feature stories on the puppeteers accompanied by 8 by 10 glossy prints with written identification of the people shown. If the sponsor is a prominent individual, give a story on him to the society page.

Your business manager should work out financial arrangements with the sponsor. He should try for a guarantee *and* a percentage, but he may have to settle for a flat guarantee or a flat percentage. Whatever the arrangement, he will sign a contract with the person in charge.

Since this is to be a mobile unit, transportation is a consideration. It will depend, no doubt, upon what is available. It can be done with several cars, preferably one with a trailer to haul the puppet theater. A luggage rack on top of a car will do if there is a cover to protect the theater from inclement weather. The drawback is that this arrangement necessitates awkward lifting. A small delivery truck or station wagon would be convenient. Whichever method of transportation is used, be certain that someone is responsible for keeping it in good running order. If you hope to be booked for return engagements, be dependable. Be on time.

Chapter 12.

The Play

You will be influenced in the choice of a play by the things a hand puppet can do. Having put the rollicking little comedian through his paces many times and knowing his capabilities, you might build the play around his type of action. The serenading skit (pp. 165) grew out of the hand-puppet's ability to carry objects and play instruments. This is a good way to develop a play if it is not one continual display of difficult actions.

Your choice of a play may be influenced by the puppet's ability to do things denied humans, such as flying or turning into other creatures. Since puppets are not limited to human forms, your play could deal with imaginative creatures such as the moon mini's in "The Trip to Earth" (pp. 175).

You will also be guided in your choice of a play by your audience—simple subject matter for the youngest age group, more sophisticated and longer plays for adults. The interest span varies considerably from kindergarten to the upper elementary grades. When my sixth-graders performed for the kindergarten classes, they found fifteen-minute plays long enough. They also learned that much more action must be packed into a given time than would be necessary for a play with human actors and that intermissions must be short in order to maintain story continuity.

Subject matter for the adult audience will vary according to the type of people who make up the audience. The play you give for a church group will not be appropriate for a nightclub audience. Nor will the play performed for hospitalized veterans be meaningful to a mentally disturbed or retarded group.

If this is your first production, do not choose a three-act play. One act with a simple background and a few characters that really comes off is far better than an overly ambitious undertaking that leaves the puppeteers discouraged and the audience bewildered.

Having in mind the type and length of play you wish to give, there are four possible sources—using a play especially written for puppets, adapting a play written for live theater, adapting a story or poem, or writing an original play.

Plays from the first source require the least effort if you can satisfy your needs. An increasing number of plays are being written for puppets; some are creative but many are mediocre. Check to see whether the play you have chosen is copyrighted and if you must pay a royalty. If it is copyrighted, get permission to use the material from the editor. See the Bibliography for a list of books on plays.

The second source, adapting a play written for the live theater, will seldom work for the hand puppet. Drastic simplification and cutting is always necessary. There is also the question of copyright.

Adapting a story or poem is most often done. There is a wealth of material from which to choose. The sources include fairy tales, fables, animal stories, ballads, nursery rhymes, and folk tales.

You may have to do a great deal of reading before you find what you want. Some stories will be too complicated, demand too many scene changes, have too many characters, or expect action too difficult or impossible for a hand puppet to perform.

If you like the story but feel it is too difficult for a first try, it is possible to simplify it and still carry the story line. All of the characters may not be essential, in which case they can be eliminated or combined if the necessary action and speeches are kept in the script. Backgrounds can be simplified and scenes can be cut or changed. Look elsewhere if the story demands action beyond the capacity of the puppet. This is generally an insurmountable obstacle.

A seventh-grade class was casting about for material for a short play. In the book *Tales of Ancient India*, by J.A.B. Buitenen, they read "The Transposed Heads," which intrigued them. Briefly, the story was this: A young wife, her husband, and her brother visited the Temple of the White Goddess to pay homage. The husband entered first. So great was his religious zeal that he decided to please the goddess with the greatest sacrifice of all, his life. He tied his head by the hair to the bell rope; then he severed it from his body with a sword.

The brother entered the temple and upon seeing his slain brother-in-law, killed himself with the same sword.

When the young woman entered and saw her dead

husband and brother, she collapsed. When she rose, she beseeched the goddess to restore her loved ones to her in her afterlife. Whereupon, she placed a rope around her neck and was about to hang herself when the voice of the goddess commanded her to join the heads and bodies that they might be made whole. She did this, but in her distraught frame of mind, she did not look closely and transposed heads and bodies. The story ends by asking which of the two mixed-up men was her husband.

The class agreed that considerable dexterity would be required of the puppets. Could a puppet tie his hair to a rope? After an unsuccessful attempt the answer was "no." The head must be tied to the rope and the sword attached to the hand while the curtain was down. Could the puppet appear to cut off his own head? The answer was "yes," but the head not attached to a rope would fall, very possibly off the playboard. Could the brother remove the sword from the husband's hand? The answer was "no"; a sword must be attached offstage. Could the wife put heads and bodies back together? The answer was "yes," very easily, but she could not put a noose around her own neck. She would have to pick it up while telling what she intended doing. All in all the class believed that they could iron out the mechanical difficulties, but when confronted with the question, "Will younger children enjoy and understand this play?" they were dubious. A rather lengthy explanation would be necessary before the play began, to shed light on the manners and morals of the people of India. The class decided to look further for a play. "But it would have been fun to make Indian heads and costumes," said one.

"I was counting on painting the white goddess with her eighteen arms on the backdrop," another confided.

This story is typical of the changes and adjustments necessary when a story is adapted for puppet performance.

When you have finally chosen a play, look over the cast of characters. Are they all needed? If not, eliminate those not necessary. Make a list of characters with descriptions of their physical characteristics, manner of speaking, and costumes. Study the story until you understand each character. Then write a simple version of the story, if necessary, breaking it into scenes and acts.

Writing the dialogue comes next. This is the most difficult part of playwriting. Dialogue must be highly concentrated with every word helping to advance the plot. At the same time speech should sound natural, not stilted.

Generally, stories must be simplified, but in the case of nursery rhymes, the simple situations must be expanded. Children's fertile imaginations will embroider with pleasure on the original story.

Let us see what happens to:

> Little Jack Horner sat in a corner
> Eating his Christmas pie,
> He stuck in his thumb
> And pulled out a plum,
> And said, "What a good boy am I."

If the teacher asks the question, "Why do you suppose Jack was sitting in the corner?" there will be as many reasons offered as there are children.

Assume his mother said, "Jack, dear, would you mind sitting in the corner? I have just seated the guests for Christmas dinner and there isn't enough room for everyone."

"No, Mother, I don't mind; I think it would be fun. Can Toby sit with me?"

"If you wish," said Mother. Jack whistles and in comes his dog who sits down beside Jack.

Mother goes offstage and returns with a pie. She bends down and gives it to Jack, who says, "Oh boy, my favorite pie!"

At this stage the teacher may say to the children, "What do you suppose a dog would do when he sees something to eat?" "Bark," some of them will say.

So Toby barks and Jack says, "No, Toby, you must wait until after dinner, then Mother will give you the scraps."

Jack looks down at his pie and says, "Look at the big plum in the middle," whereupon he sticks in his thumb (there's a common pin sewed into the thumb from the inside). He spears the plum, which is a round styrofoam ball crayoned purple. If the plum is cut flat on the bottom it will be easier to spear.

At this point the teacher should ask, "What will we do if the plum falls off onto the floor?" Someone will say, "He can ask his mother to give him another one." So Jack sticks in his thumb; if it stays on he will say, "Look at the big plum. What a good boy am I." If it falls off he will say, "Oh, oh, I dropped my plum but I'm sure Mother will give me another one." Toby sniffs the plum (audibly) as the curtain goes down.

This is a simple play but it requires careful planning. You may prefer to experiment with sticky paper attached to Jack's hand instead of the pin. The pie dish must not be slippery on the outside or it may slip from the hands of the puppet. It might be necessary to glue pieces of cloth or felt to the sides to insure a good grip. The difficulty is in manipulating the pie. It will require children with good coordination.

A one-act play calling for less dexterity could be worked out with "Little Miss Muffet."

> Little Miss Muffet
> Sat on a tuffet
> Eating her curds and whey.
> Along came a spider
> And sat down beside her
> And frightened Miss Muffet away.

When the curtain rises Miss Muffet is sitting on a tuffet. (A tuff is a rock; a tuffet must be a diminutive rock or stone.) Seat her on anything you please, but make it something firm. She holds a bowl in her two hands. Have her seated close to the outer edge of the playboard where she can be easily seen by all of the audience.

Miss Muffet sighs heavily and says, "I'm very tired; I've been playing all afternoon with Mary and her little lamb. He's cute. We ran and ran he followed us." She looks down at the dish in her hands, then looks up at the audience and says, "Do you like curds and whey?" The response from some children will surely be, "What are they?" and she answers, "Curds are what cheese is made of; they come in little chunks. Whey is also part of milk. I like curds and whey. I think I will eat."

At this point a black spider is let down from above on a thread. It can be one of the rubbery "creepy crawlers" from the dime store or a paper spider made with pipe cleaner legs. Miss Muffet screams as she rises from the stone. The dish falls from her hands as she exits screaming.

The involvement of the audience is good. Children enjoy talking with puppets. They feel close to them through this contact. It is a part of their make-believe world.

Nursery rhymes and poems can also be slowly chanted by the class while puppets pantomime the action.

Since the dramatization of nursery rhymes does not take more than five minutes, several can be given with jokes, riddles, and songs as fillers. Make use of the children's special talents with the puppets as performers.

Children can do a quiz show with puppets taking turns asking questions. If the class fails to come up with the right answer, it is supplied by the puppet. This quiz could be used to test children on subjects such as history or nature.

Problems common in family and in school can be dramatized by puppets. Children will recognize themselves when they see puppets who won't share toys, neglect pets, say "buy me this and buy me that," won't wait their turn, won't pick up books or toys, are whiners, show-offs, tattlers, or run in corridors.

The extemporaneous play is especially suited to the young actor. Here again, the imagination can go into high gear. Make a list of locations such as the zoo, on the moon, on a farm, in the woods, in a haunted house, or on a bus. Have the children form groups or teams, and give them a few minutes to plot the action. It is surprising how easily lively situations develop and how the conversation flows. This is a satisfactory type of show for the young audience; they do not demand a "finished" performance.

Adults who are performing for the young audience will be able to use any of the above-mentioned material, but it is more difficult to find material for the adult audience.

Fairy tales, folk tales, and ballads can be satirized with hilarious results. Watch TV for ideas. *The Princess and the Pea,* done with live actors, could have been done with hand puppets.

The most easily rendered and flexible type of show is the variety show into which almost anything can be incorporated. Dances, jokes, riddles, impersonations, musical numbers, songs, anecdotes, or prizefights, whatever the puppeteers have to offer, can be used. While some acts, such as the piano player, have been overworked by professional puppeteers, amateur performers will find their audiences very responsive to such a performance.

We come to the writing of an original play. This can be a very rewarding experience for children and adults.

In several children's classes we reversed the usual procedure of writing a play and then making the puppet actors. Each child wanted a puppet, so we ended up with as varied a group of characters as could be imagined. One-third were animals. The class split up in groups with one or two animals in most groups.

Television's influence on the choice of subjects for their plays was pronounced. Subject matter ranged from secret-agent tales to animal cartoons.

One group scuttled the idea of an original play because of the resemblance of one of their puppets to Little Red Riding Hood. They weren't daunted by the duck puppet in their midst; he, instead of the traditional woodcutter, rescued Little Red Riding Hood, an arrangement that was satisfactory to the young audience, judging by its applause.

Because all too few plays have been written for adult audiences, it may be necessary to write your own play.

Your idea for the play may come from any of a number of sources. If you wish to deal with the present, consider a visit to the moon or a satire on a political situation or some other aspect of the social scene. Humor, so suitable to the hand puppet, is everywhere—the home, the office, and the classroom. Human beings are at their funniest when all "shook-up" about something trivial. You could start with a situation that causes you to be happy, sad, or frightened—an incident in a restaurant, department store, or on a street corner.

If you build your play around a person, ask yourself these questions:

1. What is this person striving to get?
2. What keeps him from getting it?

3. What does he do about the obstacle?
4. What are the results of his action?
5. What is the outcome?

If you can answer these questions, you have plotted your play. A plot consists of an apparently insoluble problem with an ingenious solution.

In other words, there is conflict, an urgent *must* with an obvious *cannot*. It can be a conflict between two or more people, a person and his conscience, or a person and the elements; it may be a conflict against socially accepted behavior. Conflict is constantly present in our lives.

When you have worked out the plot to your satisfaction, consider the characters. Determine how many are necessary to the development of the plot. Since puppet characters cannot be complex, each will exhibit one invariable trait. If he is greedy, his greed will color all of his actions. If he is a black-hearted scoundrel, he will always behave like the renegade he is, likewise a noble, courageous character will be a hero always. Know each character so well that you know how he will behave in any situation.

Writing dialogue for the original play will not differ from writing it for an adaptation. It bears repeating that brevity is the keyword. Speech must be telescoped.

Dialogue must move the story. When the characters talk, there must be a reason—no idle chit-chat. They must characterize themselves, interpret the background, expose motives, help to create atmosphere, develop the plot, or convey necessary information.

Getting the necessary information to the audience

can be troublesome. A common method is to have two characters on the stage when the curtain rises who, through reminiscing or gossiping, divulge the needed facts. The conversation should arouse curiosity. It must not drag on and on. Puppets should not make long speeches. Their static expressions make it difficult to hold the spectators' interest. Long speeches should be broken up with a bit of action or with short remarks by other puppets.

Chapter 13.

Play:

"Hunting Hoax"

Characters

Cave Man—Cliff Feldspar
Wife—Flora Feldspar
Wife's Friend—Eartha Quake

Time: Stone Age
Setting: The area in front of a cave

Scene I.

At rise: (Cliff Feldspar is sitting with his back against a rock, head bent forward, sleeping. He is snoring gently. Flora emerges from the cave on the right and stands looking down at her husband.)

Flora: (indignantly) Cliff Feldspar! (Cliff jerks awake and looks up at Flora.) You are enough to try anyone's patience. Here you are sleeping when we don't know where our next meal is coming from. My dress is falling apart. (She throws her hand out and looks down at fur dress.) The fur robe on our bed is motheaten and your suit is a disgrace. (She points at husband.)

Cliff: (Stands up) Gee, Flora, I'm all tired out from painting that hunting scene on the living room wall; besides, the game is all hunted out around here.

Flora: That mural was finished days ago. You promised me a saber-tooth necklace and I told the girls at the cavemakers club that you were giving me one. My birthday is next week, so you had better get busy.

Cliff: Okay, okay, I'll go hunting, but the game is scarce. I can't tell you when I've seen a mammoth or mastodon; you might as well forget them.

Flora: I'd be happy to. Just bring home a saber-tooth tiger.

Cliff: I think the game has moved south. If I don't get anything on this trip, we will pack up and move south.

Flora: (wailing and shaking) Oh, no, Cliff. I don't want to move away from here. This is the first split level home we ever had and you just finished our mural. Besides, I don't want to leave my good friend Eartha Quake. (Flora bends her head and sobs, shaking all over.)

Cliff: Now, Flora, you needn't take on so. I'll get going on that hunting trip. (He goes over to Flora and kisses her, then exits left.)

Flora: (waves and calls) Be careful, Cliff. (She turns to the audience.) I think I'll go over and tell my friend Eartha the bad news about our moving. (Turns and looks at stage right.) Oh, here she comes now. (Eartha enters.)

Eartha: You've been crying, Flora. What is the matter?

Flora: Cliff just told me we would have to move if he doesn't bring back any big game. He just left on a three-day hunt.

Eartha: Oh, that is bad news. I don't want you to leave. Why does Cliff always go so far away to hunt? The other men hunt around here and don't complain.

Flora: Oh, you know, the grass is always greener on the other side of the fence. I wish we could think of some way of keeping him here.

Eartha: (Very excited, jumps up and down.) I've got it, I've got it!

Flora: What have you got?

Eartha: Cliff would stay here if he thought there was really big game, wouldn't he?

Flora: Of course he would, but how can we convince him there is?

Eartha: If he saw huge tracks he would believe it, wouldn't he?

Flora: (Nods) Yes, but there are no huge tracks.

Eartha: We will make a big clay leg and foot, and bake it in the fire to dry it; then we will make footprints in the wet ground, near big pond.

Flora: Oh, Eartha, that sounds wonderful. I believe it will work. Let's get started at once. (They exit right.)

Curtain

Scene II.

At rise: (Flora and Eartha enter from the right. Flora carries a large animal leg. She grunts and walks as though it is very heavy. They stop in front of the cave entrance.)

Flora: I'll take this in the cave and hide it. Cliff may be along any minute. (She goes into the cave, then returns without the leg. While she is gone, Eartha walks around and hums in a satisfied way.)

Eartha: Didn't we make beautiful tracks?

Flora: We certainly did. You are very clever, Eartha. (She puts hand to ear as though listening.) I think I hear Cliff coming. (Cliff enters from left with a small animal held by the tail in one hand, a spear in the other.)

Flora: (runs to cliff) Oh, Cliff, you are home safe and you did get an animal.

Cliff: You call this an animal? (He holds animal up for all to see.) Why, I could eat it in one bite. I'm disgusted. Tomorrow we leave for good. I suppose I'll have to skin this sorry excuse for game. (Cliff exits left. Flora and Eartha move closer together and talk in confidential tones.)

Flora: I can hardly wait to see if it works.

Eartha: It will work, you will see. Those are very convincing tracks. (Cliff returns minus animal and spear.)

Eartha: I must go home; walk a little way with me, Flora. It will be the last time we can be together.

Flora: (sadly) I know, and I feel like crying. (Flora and Eartha exit right.)

Cliff: This has been a hard three days. I think I'll take a little nap. (He sits down in front of the rock and leans back. He drops his head to his chest and in a second is snoring. There are excited calls offstage right.)

Flora: Cliff. Cliff. (The two women burst on stage. They are puffing from exertion and excitement.)

Flora, cont'd.: You will never believe what we just saw. (Cliff jumps up.)

Cliff: Well, why all of the excitement? What did you see?

Flora: (still heaving and puffing) We saw—we saw tracks, huge tracks, down near big pond. They were fresh tracks, Cliff.

Cliff: (very excited) Tracks? What kind of tracks?

Eartha: We don't know, but they are the biggest I ever saw in my life.

Cliff: (running around this way and that way) My spear, my spear, where is it?

Flora: (running up to Cliff) Think, Cliff, where did you have it last? Did you have it when you returned from hunting?

Cliff: Of course I did. Now I know. (He dashes off stage left, returns with the spear, rushes across the stage and exits right. The woman look at one another and double up with laughter.)

Eartha: Oh, Flora, this is too good to be true. He fell for it hook, line, and sinker.

Flora: Wasn't he excited?

Eartha: He will probably come back when he loses the track in dry ground, but you can be sure he'll start out again tomorrow.

(There is a great commotion off stage right, sounds of struggle, grunts, roars, whacks. The women huddle together trembling.)

Eartha: What can that be? (The noise continues.)

Flora: I don't know. Oh, I hope Cliff isn't in danger. (The noise stops. There is silence for a moment. Steps are heard above, a grinding, grating sound. Cliff enters dragging a huge animal. Both women faint.)

Curtain

Production Notes

Characters: Three hand-puppets. Give one woman long blond hair, the other black or brown hair. The man's hair is slightly shorter but ragged looking.

Costumes: The puppets' basic costumes are as close to the face color as possible to resemble bare skin. Cliff could have slightly darker skin. Each puppet wears a fur garment that is fastened on one shoulder. (See photo section.)

Properties: The stone against which Cliff sleeps is a real stone. The spear is a thin, 6-inch-long stick, with a cardboard spearhead glued to the top. The fingers are bent across the stick and pinned in place with a straight pin that can be easily removed offstage. The small animal is made of a piece of fur 5 inches by 4 inches sewn into a tube making a 2-inch-by-5-inch body and head. The head is formed by tying a string or thread tightly around the body 1 inch from top. Sew on feet, ears, and legs of felt, and attach a small animal tail or strip of fur. The large animal can be cut out of fake fur or cloth in two parts, sewn together and stuffed. It might have tusks or horns. It can be dragged in by the tail. The animal leg is made of the sawdust and wallpaper paste mixture.

Scenery: The backdrop hangs six inches from the

playboard. The cave painted on the right hand side has an opening cut into it so that puppets can enter and exit. Hang a black backdrop 6 or 8 inches behind the painted drop to give depth to the cave. Paint a fire burning beside the cave for atmosphere.

Lighting: No special effects.

Special sound effects: As a large brown paper bag is crumpled in the hands for the crackling of bushes and trees, slap a book down onto the table. At the same time someone produces the grunts, roars, and shouts.

Chapter 14.

Play:

"Fisherman's Luck"

Characters

Fisherman—Jack
Shell Collector: Tom
Camera Bug: Bill

Time: A summer morning.

Setting: On the bank of a lake.

At rise: (Jack is sitting on a rock with his back partly turned to the audience. He has a fishpole in his hand, which he flicks up and down occasionally.)

Jack: I'd better catch a fish before I go home or my wife won't believe I was fishing. (He flicks the line out of the water as he looks up.) I've still got bait on the hook. (Whistling is heard offstage right. Tom enters. Jack turns toward him.)

Tom: Well, if it isn't the old fisherman. Any luck?

Jack: None yet, but I've had a few nibbles. What are you doing so early in the morning, as if I didn't know.

Tom: Yes, I'm looking for shells. It takes a storm to wash up a new crop. (He crosses over to Jack and bends over with a hand outstretched as though to show him a shell.)

Jack: That is a very pretty one, Tom. (Tom looks offstage left.) Here comes Bill. (Bill enters. He has a camera on a strap around his neck.)

Tom and Jack: Hi, Bill!

Tom: I see the shutterbug is at work.

Bill: You bet. This is a good day for picture-taking. (He bends his head back and looks up.) Did you ever see such billowy clouds? (He looks at Jack.) I think I'll take a picture of you fishing, Jack. Pull out a big one now so I can sell the picture to *Meadow and Stream*.

Jack: No kidding, there are some really big fish in this lake.

Tom: All of six inches, I'll bet.

Bill: (Moves over in position to take the pictures. He bends his head down to look at the camera and puts both hands around it, or he can bring the camera up to his eye. A click is heard.) There. I took your picture, Jack. If you need proof that you were fishing, I have it.

Jack: (Laughing) I may need it. (He flicks his pole up and down. During the picture-taking, Tom has been walking around and bending down, hand outstretched as though he is picking up shells.)

Bill: What did you find, Tom? (They move toward one another. Tom shows Bill a shell. While they are bending over the shell with their backs to Jack, a very large fish jumps partly out of the water.)

Jack: Hey, you fellows, did you see that fish?

Tom: I suppose it was one of those big ones you told us about.

Jack: It sure was.

Bill: Stand over here, Tom, I'm going to take your picture. (Bill points.) He puts both hands around the camera and bends his head forward.) A little to the left, please, and look at the shell. (At this point the big fish jumps partly out of the water again with its mouth wide open. It grabs Jack by his free hand. Jack pulls back.)

Jack: (Yelling) Help! Help! (Tom and Bill look at Jack.)

Tom: We're coming. (Tom and Bill rush to Jack. They grab hold of him and pull back; Jack continues to yell. The fish lets go and sinks from sight with a splash.)

Jack: Whew! That was a close call. How about it, Tom? Do you think that there are big fish in this lake?

Tom: Only slightly smaller than a whale.
Curtain

Production Notes.

Characters: Three men. Give each a different hair coloring and manner of speaking.

Costumes: Give one a costume with a turtle neck to look like a sweater, another a plaid shirt, and the third one a striped shirt.

Properties: A small container such as a detergent bottle cap with a wire handle to place beside the fisherman. The fishpole is a 6-inch long thin stick with a heavy thread or string waxed to give it body. The hook must be heavy enough so that the line can be whipped back and forth without tangling. A piece of bent wire will do. Use a real rock

FIG. 56

for the fisherman's seat. The camera is a small block of wood painted black except for the round lens in front which can be wood color. A heavy piece of string or yarn fastened to either side of the camera goes around the puppet's neck. The fish is a sock puppet described on page 43.

Scenery: The backdrop should be painted with the top two-thirds blue sky and billowy white clouds and the bottom third water. Have the backdrop 1 foot from the playboard.

Special sound effects: For the sound of a camera clicking, touch a pencil point down sharply on a piece of wood or metal. For splashing water, slap a hand down into a pail of water.

Lighting: No special effects.

Chapter 15.

Play:

"Dampened Hopes"

Characters

Lovesick Youth
His loved one
Her father

Time: Late night

Setting: A street scene

At rise: (Youth with an accordion enters left. He
walks to the middle of the stage and looks up at
at the window of his love. He begins to play and
sing. Lights appear in several windows on the
street. After a little more serenading, the shutters
on the high middle window are pushed open and
a girl leans out and looks down, clasping her hands
in ecstasy. The youth looks up, sees her, then
looks back at the street. He continues to sing and
play. Suddenly the girl is yanked away from the
window and her father appears in a nightcap and

nightgown. He looks down at the young man, who does not see him. The father withdraws, then ap-appears with a container full of water, which he pours on the young man and withdraws. The youth leaps and looks up, sees nothing. Sadly, slowly, with head down, he walks offstage.)

Curtain

Production Notes

Characters: Father can be any type of character that is humorous. He could have whiskers, a goatee or eyeglasses on the end of his nose. The girl has bangs and long blond hair. The young man also has light hair which will show up on the blue-lighted stage. His head must be waterproofed with a fixative since water will be poured on him. The clothes will dry.

Costumes: Father has a white nightgown and long pointed nightcap that hangs to one side. The girl wears a frilly, light-colored nightgown. Youth is also dressed in a light color, a sweater with a slightly darker band below to suggest trousers. Since he will be standing most of the time, he could be made with legs.

Properties: The accordion is made of paper and card-board. Cut two 2½-inch square pieces of heavy cardboard. Cut three 2-inch by 7-inch strips of heavy paper. Mark them into ½-inch sections and

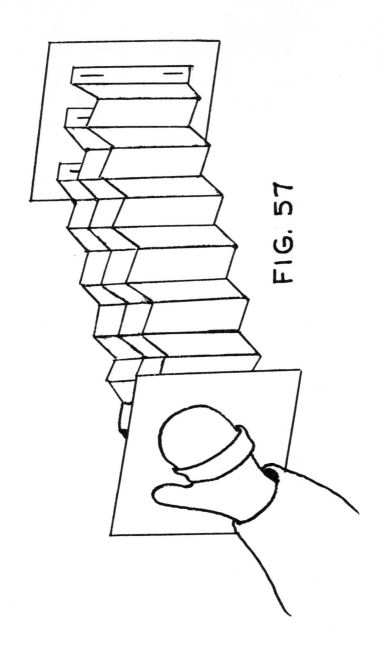

FIG. 57

accordion pleat each one. If the paper used is heavy and creases well, one thickness will do; if not, two thicknesses of construction paper glued together after pleating works well. For this you will need six instead of three strips. Staple the three accordioned strips between the square cardboards. The puppet's hands are sewn to the cardboard ends or are slipped through straps attached to outside surface of the cardboard.

The container for water can be anything that holds two or three tablespoons of water—a doll pitcher, a pressurized can cover, or small bottle covered with paper.

Scenery: The backdrop is painted to look like one side of a street. The girl's house is in the middle (for better visibility). The houses must be as tall as possible to bring the upper window above the young man's head. Several windows can be cut out, they might even have cellophane window panes and curtains. The girl's window has two shutters that open to either side.

Lighting: The stage is lighted with blue light (not too dark) to simulate night. A floodlight backstage, when turned on, will produce lights in the windows. Tie yellow cellophane over the lens.

Music: Either an accordion player or a record can furnish music to accompany the singing. See pp. 129-130 for suggested music.

Chapter 16.

Play:
"The Bear and
the Honey Bucket"

Characters

Billy Bear
Rollie Raccoon
Benny Beaver
Grandpa Fox
Blue Jay (offstage)

Time: Midday

Setting: A woods

At rise: (Billy Bear enters left looking this way and
that way. He spies a bucket beneath a tree and
ambles over to it. He bends down and sniffs
loudly.)

Billy B.: Honey, oh my! I wish there was more of it.

169

There is only a little in the bottom. I must have scared the man away before he got the honey out of this bee tree. (Looks up right.) I hear someone coming. (Rollie Raccoon enters.)

Rollie R.: What have you there, Billy Bear?

Billie B.: (pointing to bucket): A honey-bucket, Rollie.

Rollie R.: You had better eat it as fast as you can. Blue Jay just flew down the tall pine tree. He says there are hunters and dogs coming this way. I can hear them now. (Far off sound of hounds baying and guns popping.)

Billy B.: I'll eat it now. It won't take long. (He leans down and puts his head in the bucket, and speaks in muffled voice.) Rollie, I'm stuck, I'm stuck. (Straightens up with bucket on his head. He uses hands to try to get the bucket off.) Please help me, Rollie.

Rollie R.: Oh my, oh my, what can I do? (Jumps up and down.) I know, I'll get help. Oh, here comes Benny Beaver; he will help.

Benny B.: (enters right) What happened? (Billy Bear is making muffled sounds inside of the bucket and dancing around.)

Rollie R.: Billy Bear has his head stuck in this honey bucket (points) and can't get it out. Will you help me?

Benny B.: I have sharp teeth; I will gnaw it off.

Rollie R.: There isn't time. Do you hear those hounds? (Baying sounds closer.) Blue Jay says they are coming this way.

Billy B.: (muffled) Help me. Help me. (Grandpa Fox enters right.)

Grandpa Fox: What's going on here? Don't you know that the hunters and dogs are close by? We'd better clear out fast.

Billy B.: (muffled) Please don't leave me. Do something.

Benny B.: You are smart, Grandpa Fox. Can you think of a way to get Billy's head out of the bucket? (Fox walks around, head down in thought. He stops suddenly.)

Grandpa Fox: I've got a solution. Lead Billy over to the tree, Rollie. (Rollie puts a hand on Billy and helps him to the tree.)

Grandpa Fox: We will wedge the bucket in this tree

crotch and then pull Billy loose. (Fox guides bucket into crotch. Hounds bay closer; shots are heard.)

Billy B.: (muffled) Hurry, oh hurry, please.

Grandpa Fox: Now, everyone pull. (Bear's head is freed from the bucket.)

Billy B.: Whew! Am I glad to be free again.

Blue Jay: (offstage) Hurry, hurry, the hunters are almost here. (Everyone scurries offstage. There is a loud banging of guns and baying of hounds.)
Curtain

Production Notes

Characters: Four hand puppets: bear, beaver, raccoon and fox. Beaver, raccoon and fox could have tails. These are upright walking animals (see pp. 36).

Costumes: Must be light enough to show up against the dark background. Costumes can be made of cloth or fur fabric.

Properties: Tree. Make the tree of a wire foundation padded with cotton and wrapped with light brown crepe paper. A real tree branch could be used if the proper crotch could be found. The crotch must be the exact height so the puppet can lodge the bucket in it firmly.

Bucket: A cottage cheese carton could be used if it fits the bear's head snugly. If not, wrap a piece of lightweight cardboard around the head for a snug fit. Use this for the bucket side. Attach a bottom. Construct the bucket to withstand rough usage. Attach a small piece of tape firmly to the bottom of the bucket. When the bucket has been placed in the tree crotch, a puppeteer reaches up and holds the bucket firmly by the tab. His hand is encased in a black glove which will not show if the backdrop is black behind it.

Scenery: For this play, a see-through backdrop is necessary (pp. 87). The puppeteers stand behind a semitransparent black cloth in order to direct the bear's head into the bucket, etc. Trees painted on heavy paper are cut out and pinned to the backdrop suggesting a forest.

Lighting: No special effects.

Special Sound Effects: For the baying hounds, puppeteers can bay into cupped hands or plastic bowl for a faraway sound and remove the hands or bowl when baying close by. A pop gun can be used for shots. Muffle it for faraway shots.

Chapter 17.

Play:
"The Trip to Earth"

Characters

Two Moon Mini's
Astronaut Bill
Astronaut Tom (voice offstage)

Time: Daytime.

Setting: Surface of the moon.

At rise: (The two moon mini's climb out of a crater on the playboard and stand facing one another.)

1st Mini: I wonder if there is life on earth. (Mini's look at the earth painted on the backdrop.)

2nd Mini: I'll bet there is. There are probably wonderful creatures living there. I wish that I could go and see, don't you?

1st Mini: No, I don't believe I would (shakes head). I think it would be scary. I like it here.

2nd Mini: What do you suppose earthlings would be like?

1st Mini: I don't think they could be as smart as we are. I'm sure they wouldn't have energizing signal and invisibility buttons like we have. (He looks down and points to the colored buttons down his front.)

2nd Mini: I hear a peculiar noise, do you? (A faint whirring noise is heard.)

1st Mini: Yes, I do. What could it be? It seems to come from the sky. (The mini's look up. The noise becomes louder.)

2nd Mini: (Points up facing rear left.) There it is. It is coming this way. Do you suppose it has come from earth? (The mini's turn gradually from left to right as though watching the object cross the sky.)

1st Mini: We will soon know what it is. It is landing over there. (Points right.)

Curtain

Scene II

Time: Half an hour later.

Setting: Same as Scene I.

Rise: Mini's are standing on stage left, watching Astronaut Bill who is picking up small stones and putting them in a pail. His movements are slow, stiff, and deliberate. Now and then he stands and looks around. He does not see the Minis, who are invisible.

1st Mini: So that is what an earthling looks like. He is big, isn't he?

2nd Mini: Can you see what the other one is doing?

1st Mini: (Peering offstage right.) He is also picking up rocks. What do you suppose they will do with all of those rocks?

2nd Mini: I heard this one (points) tell the other one that they would have to gather them quickly before the time ran out. What do you think he meant by that?

1st Mini: I don't know, but I wish they would hurry and get out of here. They make me nervous. (He shudders.)

Astro. Bill: (Cups hands to mouth and calls off stage right.) Have you filled your pail, Tom? (Mini's cower together when he shouts.)

Astro. Tom (offstage): Not quite. But we must hurry.

Astro. Bill: I will.

2nd Mini: I just made up my mind and don't you try to change it.

1st Mini: How can I; you haven't told me what it is.

2nd Mini: I am going to earth with those creatures and see what it is like.

1st Mini: (Very agitated, jumps around.) You can't mean that, you simply can't. It would be very dangerous. You might not be able to get back to the moon. Then, if you couldn't charge your energizer with moon beams, you would be done for—completely. Do you hear? COMPLETELY .

2nd Mini: Don't get so excited. I've thought it all out. I'll charge my energizer for a month right now. (Pushes a button.) I overheard the earthlings say another capsule—that must be the thing they came in—will land here in a month.

1st Mini: How are you going to get aboard?

2nd Mini: I have that figured out too. I'm going to follow this one (points) to the capsule, and ride up the ladder on the pail. I will make myself very small.

1st Mini: You think of everything. I wish that you weren't so smart. Will you send a beam down as you pass over so I know you made it?

2nd Mini: I will. Oh oh. He's getting ready to leave. (Astro Bill picks up pail and walks offstage followed by the 2nd Mini who stops and waves to 1st Mini who waves back.)

1st Mini: Good luck.
Curtain

Scene III

Time: One month later.

Setting: Same as Scenes I and II.

Rise: (1st Moon Mini is standing center stage facing right with hands outstretched welcoming 2nd Mini who approaches him.)

1st Mini: Welcome home, my friend. I'm glad you made it back.

2nd Mini: Not half as glad as I am, you can be sure.

1st Mini: You don't sound very enthusiastic about your earth visit. Tell me all about it.

2nd Mini: I'll tell you but you won't believe it. First of all, those creatures that were here don't resemble earthlings at all.

1st Mini: How do they differ?

2nd Mini: Those on earth aren't as big and they are much more agile. They must have sent those big ones up to scare us.

1st Mini: What else did you see?

2nd Mini: I observed some of the strangest behavior. For one thing, earthlings are continually stuffing things in their speaking tubes, all kinds of strange things, but mostly it is what they call hot dogs and ice cream. (Mini makes motions with hands as though putting things in his mouth.)

1st Mini: Why do they do that?

2nd Mini: I think they energize that way. One of the strangest things they do is take off their covering, called clothes, put on a very scanty covering which the females call bikinis. They jump into a substance which they call water. (Motions jumping and diving.) They seem to enjoy this water.

They scream and make silly motions. (Makes swimming motions.)

1st Mini: What else did you see?

2nd Mini: They live in structures they call houses. They work in other structures. All of them are bunched together. I'm sure they do not like this because they often get into buglike contraptions and go very fast to get away. They go to places where this water is and things they call trees.

1st Mini: Tell me about the bug contraptions.

2nd Mini: All I can say is they are energized to go like lightning. Very often they run into one another. When they do, earthlings are often immobilized—from what I could observe, quite permanently. (Flops down on ground and remains quiet for a second, then jumps up.)

1st Mini: Then, I gather that you are very glad to be back.

2nd Mini: (Throws up hand.) It's a nice place to visit, but I wouldn't want to live there.
                    Curtain
(This could be the basis for an adult-level satire.)

FIG. 58

Production Notes

Characters: Three hand puppets; one stage voice (Astro Tom). The moon Mini's can take any form that you can imagine, but they should be small in comparison to the astronaut. Consider features such as antennae, horns, one eye, many arms, a tube for a mouth, long nose or pointed ears, which emphasize the difference between humans and moon Mini's.

Costumes: The astronaut is tall and bulky; make his costume of heavy white or light gray material. The helmet is a large paper drinking cup, cut down if it is too tall. The front is cut out and heavy cellophane is taped to the inside. Attach it to the costume to prevent its falling off when the astronaut bends forward. Attach a block of cellophane to his back and run tubes made of cloth from it to the front. This puppet could have legs and feet if you wish. The feet should be bulky and heavily weighted.

The mini costumes should be colorful and have several buttons down the front.

Properties: Real pebbles, a pail. This can be any container which the puppeteer can grasp between his thumb and third finger and carry. It should be large and strong enough to hold a number of small pebbles. The crater is made by modeling wallpaper-paste mixture on the outside of a cardboard that is bent to form one-half of a crater. The back side is open to allow the Mini's to enter.

Scenery: The playboard is the moon's surface. The crater helps to create that illusion. Real pebbles are strewn about. The backdrop is painted with the surface of the moon, appearing to be an extension of the playboard. The earth and clouds are painted in the sky.

Lighting: A piece of red cellophane is passed across one of the floodlights on the inside of the puppet theater to produce the light signal from the Mini in the spacecraft.

Sound: A blender started on low, then turned to high, makes the sound of the capsule arriving and leaving.

Chapter 18.

Jokes and Riddles

Jokes and riddles can be used between acts of a play or in a variety show by using a comedian and a straight man. Another way in which they can be used is to have characters pop out of doors and converse with one another.

For this you will need a piece of heavy cardboard cut to fit the stage opening. Have a row of high doors and a row of low doors. To make the doors, cut out the top, bottom, and one side of a door that is large enough so that a puppet can lean out of it. Bend the door to form a hinge. Knobs and hinges can be painted on the doors. To prevent the door from being drawn in too far when it is shut, staple a narrow strip on the inside of the opening.

Instead of cardboard, ¼-inch plywood can be used to make this setup. Hinge the doors with tiny metal hinges.

Make each puppet as unique and eye-catching as possible and give them laugh-provoking names. Have male and female puppets.

If the puppet theater is not large enough to accommodate six people as shown in Figure 59, do not have as many doors, or have them close to one another so that a puppeteer can operate a puppet on each hand.

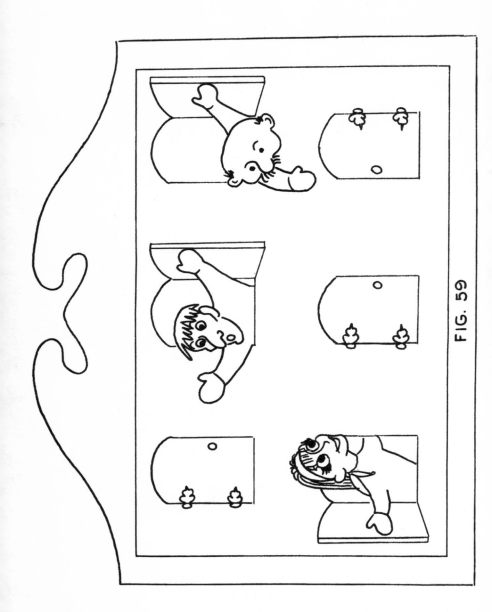

FIG. 59

If one of the puppet's hands is fastened to the inside of the door, it is automatically closed when he withdraws from the opening.

Children will enjoy using a board which has painted flowers instead of doors. Each flower has a round hole cut out of the center. The puppet pops his head out of the center of the flower.

Animal puppets might be used as well as human-type puppets. A skunk could pop out of a petunia or a skunk cabbage. The puppet that emerges from a daisy could refuse to give the answer to a riddle because "daisies won't tell."

Following is a list of riddles and jokes you might like to use:

"What is it that has four legs, has a tail, eats hay and sees just as well from one end as the other?"
"I give up."
"A blind horse."

"I'm so glad I'm not a bird."
"Why?"
"I can't fly."

"Tell me two things you can never eat for breakfast."
"I give up."
"Lunch and supper."

"I lost my dog."
"Why don't you put an ad in the paper?"
"He can't read."

"My brother and I together, we know everything in the whole world."

"Is that so? What is the square root of 144?"

"That's one my brother knows."

"Where was the Declaration of Independence signed?"

"At the bottom."

"How can you buy eggs and be sure there are no chickens in them?"

"Buy goose eggs."

"What do you call a small joke?"

"A mini ha ha."

"Have your eyes ever been checked?"

"No, they have always been brown."

"What did papa lightning bug say to mama lightning bug?"

"My, isn't junior bright for his age?"

"What do you think about Red China?"

"It looks good with a white tablecloth."

"If I had a thousand men and you had a thousand men and we were at war, who would win?"

"I give up."

"I win; you just gave up."

"Can you tell me what a canary can do that I can't?"
"I give up."
"Take a bath in a saucer."

"Seven cows are walking along a path in single file. Which one can turn around and say, 'I see six pairs of horns'."
"Why, the first cow."
"Wrong, cows can't talk."

"Is there a connecting link between the animal and vegetable kingdom?"
"Yes, man, hash."

"A man swam a river three times before breakfast each day, nude."
"Why didn't he swim it four times so he could get back to his clothes?"

"Which month has twenty-eight days?"
"They all have."

"Do you think there is intelligent life on Mars?"
"Certainly, I do. You don't see them wasting 30 billion dollars to find out if there is life on earth."

Bibliography

Arnott, Peter D.: Plays Without People. Indiana University Press, 1964.

Baird, Bil: The Art of the Puppet. The Macmillan Co., 1965.

Baranski, Mathew: Mask Making. Davis Publications, 1962.

Beaumont, Cyril W.: Puppets and the Puppet Stage. Studio Publications, 1938.

Binyon, Helen: Puppetry Today. Watson-Guptill, 1966.

Bodor, John: Creating and Presenting Hand-Puppets. Reinhold Publishing Corp., 1967.

Bufano, Remo: Remo Bufano's Book of Puppetry. The Macmillan Co.

Hopper, Grizella: Puppet Making Through the Grades. Davis Publications, 1966.

Howard, Vernon: Puppet and Pantomine Plays. Sterling Publishing Co., 1962.

Jagendorf, Moritz: The First Book of Puppets. Franklin Watts, Inc., 1952.

———: Penny Puppets. Plays, Inc. 1966.

Lewis, Roger: Puppets and Marionettes. Alfred Knopf, 1952.

McCrea, Lilian: Puppets and Puppet Plays. Oxford University Press, 1949.

MacNamara, Desmond: Puppetry. Horizon Press, 1966.

Morton, Brenda: Needlework Puppets. Fabar and Fabar, 1964.

Mulholland, John: Practical Puppetry. Arco Publishing Co., Inc., 1961.

Niculescu, Margaret: The Puppet Theatre of the Modern World, 1967.

Philpott, A. R.: Eight Plays for Hand-Puppets. Plays, Inc., 1968.

Slade, Richard: Clever Hands. Faber and Faber Ltd., 1959.

Snook, Barbara: Puppets. Charles T. Branford Co., 1965.

Tichenor, Tom: Folk Plays for Puppets You Can Make. Abingdon Press, 1959.

Tuttle, Florence Piper: Puppets and Puppet Plays. Creative Educational Society, 1962.

Van Biutenen, J. A. B.: Tales of Ancient India. University of Chicago Press, 1959.

Sources for Supplies

Art Materials: paints, brushes, paper glue, block printing materials, matte finishes

1. The American Crayon Company
   P. O. Box 2067
   Sandusky, Ohio 44870

2. Binney and Smith, Inc.
   380 Madison Ave.
   New York, N.Y. 10017

Materials, such as glitter, felt cloth, burlap, spangles, glass jewels, rhinestones, covered wire, arm foam, trimmings

1. Holiday Handicrafts, Inc.
   Apple Hill,
   Winsted, Connecticut

2. Delco Craft Center, Inc.
   30084 Stephenson Highway
   Madison Heights, Mich. 48071

3. Immerman's Crafts, Inc.
   16912 Mills Ave.
   Cleveland, Ohio 44128

Records and Sounds

Publishers Central Bureau
3320 Hunter's Point Ave.
Long Island City, N.Y. 11101

Felt Mill Ends—Irregular Pieces, 3# pcs.
12-inch squares
6-inch squares

Eastern Mills
170 Third St., Box 154
Chelsea, Mass. 02150

Very useful packages of 60 assorted colors and shapes of lamb's wool and bag of exotic feather fluffs.

Dick Blick
P. O. Box 1267
Galesburg, Ill. 61401

Largest selection of sound effects

Thomas Valentine, Inc.
150 W. 46th St.
New York, N.Y. 10036

Index

NOTES

NOTES

NOTES

NOTES